No Doubt!
USC's 2004 Championship Season

SP
SPORTS
PUBLISHING
L.L.C.

www.SportsPublishingLLC.com

Hard cover ISBN: 1-59670-077-7
Soft cover ISBN: 1-59670-035-1

All stories and photographs are from the files of
the Los Angeles Newspaper Group unless otherwise noted.

Front and back cover photos: Doug Pensinger/Getty Images

Printed in the United States of America

Sports Publishing L.L.C.
804 North Neil Street
Champaign, IL 61820
Phone: 1-877-424-2665 • Fax: 217-363-2073 • Web site: www.SportsPublishingLLC.com

Daily News INLAND VALLEY Daily Bulletin PASADENA STAR-NEWS Press-Telegram
Redlands Daily Facts SAN GABRIEL VALLEY TRIBUNE THE•SUN WHITTIER DAILY NEWS

GERALD GRILLY *president and CEO*

TRACY RAFTER *publisher*

DAVID J. BUTLER *editor*

DOUG JACOBS *executive sports editor*

DEAN MUSGROVE *director of photography*

BILL VAN LANINGHAM *marketing director*

PAUL SCHRAEDER *marketing graphic designer*

PETER L. BANNON and JOSEPH J. BANNON SR.
publishers

SUSAN M. MOYER *senior managing editor*

JOSEPH J. BANNON JR. *acquisitions editor*

NOAH ADAMS AMSTADTER *coordinating editor*

DEAN MILLER
developmental editor

K. JEFFREY HIGGERSON *art director*

KENNETH O'BRIEN and JIM HENEHAN *book design*

JOSEPH BRUMLEVE *cover design*

JENNIFER POLSON *book layout*

DUSTIN HUBBART *imaging*

ERIN LINDEN-LEVY *photo editor*

KEVIN KING *vice president of sales and marketing*

NICK OBRADOVICH *regional,*
RANDY FOUTS *national,*
MAUREY WILLIAMSON *print
media and promotions managers*

Contents

Foreword

There's not much going on around USC in early August, weeks before students arrive for school, but Trojans coach Pete Carroll delivered his first lesson for the 2004 season on a quiet summer night at Howard Jones Field.

He assembled the Trojans at midfield and talked about winning the national championship. Carroll lost three assistant coaches and was missing several players expected to return in 2004, like wide receiver Mike Williams, offensive tackle Winston Justice and fullback Brandon Hancock.

But as Carroll demonstrated repeatedly at USC, he merely plugs holes and keeps moving forward, and gets the Trojans to believe in his message.

The Trojans were 13-0 in 2004, starting with an emotional 24-13 victory over Virginia Tech before more than 90,000 in Landover, Maryland, and finishing with a 55-19 rout of No. 2 Oklahoma in the Orange Bowl.

USC's 13 victories were part of a 22-game overall winning streak, the longest current winning streak in the country.

"We just take every game one at a time, that's the key to our success," tailback LenDale White said.

It's been a very good year for the Trojans, who became just the second team to be No. 1 from the preseason poll to the final poll in the Associated Press Top 25. The only other team to do it was Florida State in 1999.

There were several nail-biters, notably a come-from-behind 31-28 victory over Stanford, a 23-17 win over No. 4 Calfornia and a 29-24 victory over crosstown rival UCLA.

But it didn't matter. If one play went differently, any of those games could have been losses, but the Trojans found ways to pull out close wins.

"All of our wins last year were blowouts, this year we've shown we can win close games," quarterback Matt Leinart said.

Leinart made history too, becoming USC's sixth Heisman Trophy winner and second in the past three years. He went 25-1 as a starter and threw five touchdowns in the Orange Bowl and was named the game's MVP.

That's even more impressive considering the Trojans lost Williams (ineligible) and were without tight end Dominique Byrd and starting receiver Steve Smith because of injuries for large parts of the season.

The Trojans offense barely skipped a beat with so many starters missing. One reason was the emergence of tailback Reggie Bush, USC's most explosive player in years. Bush, who finished fifth in the Heisman voting, was named an All-American even though he didn't make his first start until the Orange Bowl.

He amassed 2,330 all-purpose yards this season, the most since Marcus Allen in 1981 and had 33 plays of 20 or more yards. Bush even threw for a touchdown this year.

"Reggie was our MVP," Leinart said. "He won games for us by himself."

Perhaps one of the more important accomplishments came when USC swept its archrivals. Carroll became the first coach in USC history to sweep Notre Dame and UCLA in three consecutive seasons.

Carroll said the secret to dominating the archrivals was not making too much about who the opponent was.

"Hard work and clear focus is how we dealt with the pitfalls and hurdles faced during the season," Carroll said. "No game is bigger than the next game. We don't rejoice after a win anymore than we should."

Except after the Orange Bowl, that is.

"These guys demonstrated they had faith in everything we did," Carroll said. "All in all, it was a great night for us."

—Scott Wolf
Staff Writer

Brian Bahr/Getty Images

Scripting Sequel to Success

By Scott Wolf, *Staff Writer*

The idea of a re-Pete around USC sounds pretty easy, especially since most preseason top-25 polls agree.

But the Trojans won't even need to leave their own conference to find skeptics regarding their chances of winning back-to-back national championships.

"I think it's practically impossible," Oregon coach Mike Bellotti said.

USC might be the overwhelming favorite to win the Pacific-10 Conference, but Bellotti doesn't think another national title is likely for the Trojans. And it might be easier to say that considering the Ducks don't face USC this season.

"Nowadays, with the parity of talent, it's difficult," Bellotti said. "Fifteen years ago, you could stockpile athletes. You can't do that today. And everyone's going for you in your conference. You'll get everyone's 'A' game."

Even Arizona State coach Dirk Koetter, who

ABOVE: Some of the new blood for the Trojans' march to a repeat national championship include Rocky Hinds (7), Dwayne Jarrett (8), Jeff Byers (53) and Jeff Schweiger (54). *Staff photo by John Lazar*

"USC deserves everything they get (in the polls), but for the other nine teams in the conference, that's everybody's big game," Koetter said. "Who isn't going to be excited to play them?

"Everyone definitely will remember it if you beat them. That's the game you remember your whole life."

Nearly everyone seems to remember the Trojans lost to California last season, their only blemish on the way to the national championship. But it has been a while since a team repeated.

The last time a team finished first in the Associated Press poll in consecutive seasons was Nebraska in 1994-95. Before that, Alabama finished atop the AP poll in 1978-79.

The coaches' poll is even pickier. Besides Nebraska in the mid-'90s, the previous repeat champion was Texas in 1969-70.

"I didn't know that stat," USC linebacker Matt Grootegoed said. "The statistics show it's hard to do that. It's a pretty prestigious accomplishment. But we don't really talk about national championships."

Silence, of course, is just the way USC coach Pete Carroll likes it. This is the same guy who went out of his way to not learn the Bowl Championship Series formula last season, even when it dominated college football debates.

So why would he mention such a daunting task as back-to-back titles? Instead, Carroll skips the historical significance of this season by merely focusing on the future.

"That kind of stuff doesn't matter," Carroll said. "We have goals that relate to this season. Afterward, if we've accomplished something, that would be great."

With that mind-set drilled into them, the Trojans tend to repeat Carroll's philosophy.

"Repeating? I'm not worried about it," linebacker Lofa Tatupu said. "It presents a challenge, but we welcome it. We've got a lot of challenges we take on, so why not take on this one while we're at it?"

Running back LenDale White admitted the players think about another title but insisted it's not an everyday topic during the preseason, when a more likely subject is the season opener against Virginia Tech on Saturday in Landover, Maryland.

"I'm pretty sure we've got thoughts, but we haven't played a game yet," White said. "Once you think too far ahead, you get caught. The national championship isn't decided until January 4.

"Personally, I'm ready for any challenge. We can step up to anything. We're unique."

If nothing else, USC's chances of repeating certainly are not hurt by its schedule. According to collegefootballnews.com, the Trojans have the nation's 33rd-toughest schedule and only the seventh-toughest in the Pac-10.

After playing Virginia Tech, USC doesn't leave the West the rest of the season, with road games against lowly Brigham Young, sinking Stanford and trips to Washington State and Oregon State in consecutive weeks, perhaps the "tough" stretch of the schedule.

A trip to Corvallis, Ore., could be difficult, though, and USC lost its last game there in 2000. But it hardly compares to playing between the hedges in Georgia or going to Death Valley at Louisiana State. Oregon State experiences both this season.

Then again, the Trojans didn't anticipate Notre Dame would be down another season or that Virginia Tech wouldn't be a top-25 team.

That doesn't faze Bellotti, however, who still thinks the schedule will be difficult.

"If they do it, it's tremendous no matter what because I think they'll have to be ready to play every game," he said.

Cody thinks the best way to claim the title is developing amnesia about 2003.

"We left that season behind. It means nothing," Cody said.

"Hopefully, we can have another magical season. That's how I'd like to go out."

Grootegoed has a personal reason for wanting another. He's missed half of last season with a torn ligament in his ankle and became frustrated over his smaller-than-expected contribution to the Trojans' success.

"I was part of the team the first half of the season, but I barely played 10 plays in the Rose Bowl. I didn't feel I did as much as I could," he said.

Perhaps Koetter also has a reason for hoping USC stumbles. The Trojans' recruiting prowess is beginning to affect everyone else, and some schools seem resigned to losing players to USC.

"The number of recruits USC wants and doesn't get has shrunk," Koetter said.

"They gave it to us for a reason. Last year, they did get us on the polls at the end of the season. But now it's a target. Everyone wants to beat us."

USC quarterback Matt Leinart claimed to be unimpressed with the initial polls.

"I could care less," Leinart said.

"But it's cool because it shows how hard we've worked. That's our goal, to be at the top."

Besides USC and Oklahoma, third-ranked Georgia received five first-place votes and LSU received one.

Real Eye Opener

By Scott Wolf, *Staff Writer*

L ANDOVER, Md.—The Heisman Trophy candidate experienced jitters. The top-ranked team in the nation trailed for the first time in 11 months. The coach grew frustrated.

No, USC wasn't the same team last seen in Pasadena on New Year's Day, and in case confirmation was a necessity, all you needed to know was the Trojans were losing to Virginia Tech, those alleged 18-point underdogs.

"It did feel different," USC coach Pete Carroll said. "And with all the hype and buildup, doubt might have crept up in somebody's mind in the locker room at halftime. They won't admit it but it did."

In true Carroll fashion, though, the doubt didn't last an entire four quarters. The Trojans regrouped and resembled the team expected to contend for the national title as they held off the Hokies 24-13 in front of 91,665 at FedEx Field in the Black Coaches Association Classic.

"They proved they can finish it off," Carroll said. "There's a lot to be gained from a close win. Nobody said you have to be your best in the first game."

USC certainly wasn't its best. And Carroll doesn't really do close wins. He tends to have blowouts or close losses.

But this game never felt right, especially when quarterback Matt Leinart uncharacteristically got nervous at the outset. Maybe not having receiver Mike Williams will do that.

Delane B. Ru??al/Icon SMI

ABOVE: LenDale White (21) led the Trojans' rushing attack with 15 carries and 78 yards.
Delane B. Rouse/Icon SMI

"I was a little shaky," Leinart said. "We were out of rhythm. A lot of anxiety built up. Maybe we were too excited."

Part of the problem was Leinart's receiving corps. With two sophomores and a freshman, routes weren't always being run properly in the first half, a problem Leinart rarely encountered with Williams and Keary Colbert.

"We weren't in the right spots a lot of times," offensive coordinator Norm Chow said.

That helped explain how the Trojans trailed 10-7 at halftime, the first time USC trailed since their double-overtime loss to California on Sept. 27.

To make matters worse, Virginia Tech quarterback Bryan Randall scrambled for 96 yards in the first half.

"We've got a lot of playmakers on defense and they had a guy making freak plays," defensive tackle Shaun Cody said.

Only a screen pass from Leinart that sophomore Reggie Bush took 35 yards into the end zone kept the Trojans from trailing by even more.

However, midway through the second half Leinart regained his composure and resumed his Heisman campaign.

"There was a point in the third quarter where he gave me a little smile," Carroll said. "He was pressing. Then he settled down and gave us a beautiful win."

The key was the Leinart-to-Bush connection—they hooked up for two more touchdowns in the second half, a 53-yarder that gave USC a 14-10 lead and a 29-yard pass play with 5:35 left that finally gave the Trojans some breathing room at 21-13.

Those two plays rescued what could have been an opener of disastrous proportions for the Trojans.

"There's more pressure when you're No. 1," linebacker Matt Grootegoed said. "That comes with the territory."

The idea of repeating as national champions certainly looked difficult against the Hokies, as the Trojans' inexperience suddenly showed at several positions, especially along the offensive line.

"I don't think you can show you're No. 1 by winning a game," offensive guard John Drake said.

Although the defense struggled at times, it avoided surrendering any back-breaking plays to Randall in the

	1	2	3	4	Score
Virginia Tech	3	7	0	3	13
USC	7	0	7	10	24

Scoring Summary

USC - Bush 35 yd pass from Leinart (Killeen kick), five plays, 47 yards in 2:35
VT - Pace 35 yd field goal, nine plays, 62 yards in 4:17
VT - Hyman 12 yd pass from Randall (Pace kick), 10 plays, 80 yards in 5:14
USC - Bush 53 yd pass from Leinart (Killeen kick), two plays, 67 yards in 0:32
VT - Pace 42 yd field goal, nine plays, 45 yards in 4:02
USC - Bush 29 yd pass from Leinart (Killeen kick), five plays, 86 yards in 2:20
USC - Killeen 41 yd field goal, four plays, three yards in 1:07

Team Statistics

	VT	USC
First Downs	18	16
Rushes-Yards (Net)	34-141	29-101
Passing-Yards (Net)	153	272
Completions-Attempts-Int	14-29-1	19-29-0
Total Offense Plays-Yards	63-294	58-373
Fumbles-Lost	1-1	3-0
Penalties-Yards	6-50	7-60
Punts-Yards	5-229	5-214
Punt Returns-Yards	1-10	4-60
Kickoff Returns-Yards	3-70	3-44
Possession Time	31:31	28:29
Sacks by (Number-Yards)	2-12	4-27

Individual Offensive Statistics

Rushing: **VT**-Randall 17-82; Hamilton 8-33; Humes 9-26.
USC-White 15-78; Bush 9-27; Smith 1-(-1); Leinart 4-(-3).

Passing: **VT**-Randall 14-29-153-1.
USC-Leinart 19-29-272-0.

Receiving: **VT**-King 4-65; Johnson 3-27; Humes 2-9; Mazzetta 1-22; Hyman 1-12; Kinzer 1-8; Clowney 1-7; Hamilton 1-3.
USC-Bush 5-127; Smith 4-68; Kirtman 3-32; Holmes 2-12; McFoy 2-11; Jarrett 2-8; Webb 1-14.

Individual Defensive Statistics

Interceptions: **VT**-None.
USC: Tatupu 1-32.

Sacks: **VT**-Tapp 1, Davis 1.
USC: Patterson 2.5; Tatupu 1; Schweiger 1; Jackson .5.

Tackles (Unassisted-Assisted): **VT**-Tapp 3-6; Anderson 2-5; Fuller 4-2; Green 3-3; Warren 3-3; Williams 2-2; Ellis 3-0; Griffin 3-0; Davis 2-1; Hall 1-2; Burchette 1-2.
USC-Tatupu 6-2; Bing 6-1; Grootegoed 4-2; Patterson 3-3; Leach 3-2; Wyatt 2-1; Sartz 1-2; Cody 1-2; Schweiger 1-2.

second half. The quarterback gained just 21 yards in the second half.

"We did a good job of figuring it out," Cody said.

It's too early to say a season was salvaged but the Trojans kept their pride intact with the victory, which appeared almost identical to their Orange Bowl victory, at least in atmosphere. Virginia Tech brought more

than 50,000 fans, with its campus just a 4-hour drive away.

And in the first half, the Hokies seemed ready to shock the college football establishment that uniformly crowned USC the nation's top team.

Leinart often was harried and forced to scramble behind his new offensive line. It was quickly apparent the Trojans missed their safety net, Williams, who often bailed out the offense last season.

The NCAA denied Williams' reinstatement Thursday and in the first half, only tailback LenDale White seemed capable of filling that role. But White is not a receiver, which deprived Leinart of a go-to player in passing situations.

Equally important was the absence of suspended right tackle Winston Justice, something the Hokies exploited repeatedly.

Without Williams or Justice, Leinart's Heisman campaign didn't exactly get off to a rousing start, as he completed eight of 16 passes for 102 yards and one touchdown in the opening half. Credit Williams' absence and four new starters on the line as the major reasons.

Leinart finished 19 of 29 for 272 yards and three touchdowns, numbers good enough to stay in the Heisman race. He's thrown 33 touchdowns and just three interceptions in his past 10 games.

There were also breakdowns defensively, a somewhat more surprising development since the Trojans returned nine starters on that side of the ball.

All of those factors reached a crescendo with 6:19 left in the half, when the Hokies took a 10-7 lead on a 12-yard pass from Randall to Josh Hyman. The halftime score made a mockery of the oddsmakers, who established USC as an 18-point favorite.

"The first win is the hardest one," Grootegoed said. "It's just nice to get it."

ABOVE: Matt Leinart launched USC's national championship aspirations with 272 yards and three touchdowns.
Delane B. Rouse/Icon SMI

BELOW: Sophomore Reggie Bush electrified Trojan fans with 263 all-purpose yards and three touchdowns.
Delane B. Rouse/Icon SMI

#79 SAM BAKER

By Scott Wolf, *Staff Writer*

Sam Baker has made left tackle the least-discussed position at USC, the only spot along the Trojans' offensive line where no one else even gets mentioned for possible playing time.

For a redshirt freshman to cruise into a top-ranked team's starting lineup without even a hint of competition is impressive under normal circumstances. But Baker has seized a job and flourished with a lot more on his mind than football. Last March, right when he first showed USC coaches he could replace All-American Jacob Rogers, Baker learned his mother was diagnosed with breast cancer. Since then, he has watched her go through chemotherapy and radiation treatments as he became a significant member of USC's football team.

"My mom's always been a stronghold for us. When I'm weak, she's strong," Baker said. "Each treatment she got weaker and weaker. She always says she's OK, but the word 'cancer' is scary."

The toughest moment for Baker was the day his mom, Patty, asked him to shave her head after her hair began falling out from chemotherapy.

"That's the one time it really hit me," Baker said.

Although he intended to let his hair grow out this season, Baker is keeping his head shaved as a tribute to his mother.

"As long as she's bald, I'm going to keep mine this way," he said.

Although he lives at USC, Baker commuted to Tustin during the summer to get his mom's prescriptions and be there for her.

"He had summer school but would come home every day," Patty Baker said. "I definitely relied on him a lot. My biggest concern is that he wouldn't worry. I talked to him every night.

"He's very easy-going but sensitive too and quiet and shy. A lot of times, what he feels, he doesn't say anything about."

During training camp, a critical time for a redshirt freshman who never has started, Baker was more worried about the fact he couldn't go home and see his mom.

"We were locked down in camp and she was getting chemo treatments," Baker said. "That was hard for me."

It didn't make things easier for Patty, either, because she didn't want her son to worry.

"Just because it's an important time in (his) life, you don't want to distract him," she said.

Even with the cancer treatments, Patty has achieved her goal of going to all USC games, home and away. She even made the Virginia Tech trip in late August, when she was still undergoing chemotherapy.

Despite the situation, Baker has been perhaps the brightest spot along the offensive line. He has allowed just one sack and been a mainstay, whereas players have alternated at nearly every other position.

"He's one of those guys athletically who's really at the forefront," offensive line coach Tim Davis said. "He rarely makes mistakes and he could potentially be better than Jacob Rogers because of how early he's matured."

Baker is a "perfectionist" according to Davis, and that's one reason he gives himself mixed reviews when analyzing his performance.

"It's been kind of up and down," Baker said. "I kind of know how I'm doing, if I'm having good games or bad games. The Cal game I had a real tough game. I just came out real slow. It was one of those days."

Davis wasn't worried about the Cal game. He said Baker "didn't play as well as he should have, but he fixed it."

And he'll only get better. He's on course to be a four-year starter at tackle, something that rarely happens in college football.

"That's a big responsibility. I don't know if I anticipated it," Baker said. "It's pretty cool that it happened like this because left tackle is a tough position. In practices, I take all the reps and I look around and see other guys rotating at the other positions."

If Baker's tough on himself, he can always turn to Patty for reinforcement, although she admits being slightly awed by his situation.

"It hasn't sunk in he plays for the No. 1 team in the nation," she said.

Patty said Sam's quiet nature mirrors her own personality.

Frequently, stories on Sam revolve around his father and her former husband, David Baker, the commissioner of the Arena Football League.

"I don't really prefer the attention," she said.

Sam added: "My mom thinks the coaches don't even know who she is."

Class: *Redshirt Freshman*
Hometown: *Tustin, California*
High School: *Tustin*
Major: *undecided*
Position: *Offensive Tackle*
Height: *6'5"*
Weight: *290*

Staff photo by Andy Holzman

Progressing to Last Year

BY SCOTT WOLF, *STAFF WRITER*

USC silenced the doubters and critics who questioned whether the Trojans deserved their No. 1 ranking, simply by looking into the mirror.

Whatever anyone else said, the Trojans were the ones unhappy with their season-opening victory over Virginia Tech and defensive tackle Shaun Cody called a players-only meeting to make sure everyone knew it.

"I don't want guys to think because we won that we played good," Cody said.

Quarterback Matt Leinart added: "We wanted the attitude and hunger like last year."

There were no complaints in the locker room Saturday night, as the Trojans routed Colorado State 49-0 in front of 85,521 at the Coliseum.

"People wondered, 'How good are they? Did they gain a step or lose a step?'" offensive lineman John Drake said. "We made a statement. At least for one game."

This was the way USC (2-0) won games last season and the way it was expected to win by the rest of the country.

Staff photo by Evan Yee

Quarterback Matt Leinart performed in Heisman-candidate style, completing 20 of 31 passes for 231 yards and two touchdowns, and tailback LenDale White rushed for 123 yards and two touchdowns.

More importantly, some of the unknowns emerged. Receiver Steve Smith led the Trojans with eight receptions for 79 yards and the defense looked much better than in the opener.

The Trojans intercepted four passes, including two by linebacker Matt Grootegoed, and received inspired efforts from freshman defensive end Jeff Schweiger and cornerback Justin Wyatt.

It even helped calm the head man, as USC coach Pete Carroll expressed relief after the resounding performance.

"This is really what we hoped for. A complete game at the Coliseum in front of a big crowd," Carroll said. "I feel a lot more connected at what we're capable of doing after tonight's game."

Translation: Carroll won't be up quite as late at night wondering what would happen if Mike Williams, Kenechi Udeze and Winston Justice still were around.

A perfect example was Schweiger, who couldn't remember to bring his mouthpiece out of the locker room two weeks ago at Virginia Tech and didn't see the field until the third quarter.

He played in the first quarter Saturday and finished with four tackles, a sack, a forced fumble and 2.5 tackles for loss.

"I didn't question myself like the last game," Schweiger said. "It's definitely a different atmosphere now."

Part of the difference for Schweiger was the team meeting, which introduced first-year players to the high expectations that exist within the team.

LEFT: Reggie Bush breaks away for some of his 84 rushing yards during the game against Colorado State. *Staff photo by Evan Yee*

	1	2	3	4	Score
Colorado State	0	0	0	0	0
USC	7	21	14	7	49

Scoring Summary
USC - White 11 yd run (Killeen kick), 12 plays, 92 yards in 4:42
USC - White 1 yd run (Killeen kick), two plays, 32 yards in 0:14
USC - White 3 yd run (Killeen kick), seven plays, 74 yards in 3:14
USC - Bush 7 yd run (Killeen kick), nine plays, 96 yards in 3:25
USC - Smith 5 yd pass from Leinart (Killeen kick), nine plays, 64 yards in 2:47
USC - Jarrett 4 yd pass from Leinart (Killeen kick), three plays, 25 yards in 1:12
USC - Wright 20 yd fumble recovery (Killeen kick)

Team Statistics

	CS	USC
First Downs	14	32
Rushes-Yards (Net)	27-48	45-322
Passing Yards (Net)	233	231
Passes Att-Comp-Int	35-19-4	31-20-0
Total Offense Plays-Yards	62-281	76-553
Fumble Returns-Yards	0-0	1-20
Punt Returns-Yards	1-1	5-19
Kickoff Returns-Yards	6-110	1-39
Punts (Number-Avg)	7-43.1	4-43.2
Fumbles-Lost	3-2	3-2
Penalties-Yards	7-45	7-60
Possession Time	26:47	33:13
Sacks by (Number-Yards)	0-0	4-44

Individual Offensive Statistics
Rushing: **Colorado State**-Jaunarajs 13-74; Walker 3-12; Houston 5-1; Holland 6-(-39). **USC**-White 14-123; Bush 12-84; Reed 8-56; Leinart 7-46; Kirtman, David 3-17; Hance 1-(-4).

Passing: **Colorado State**-Holland 19-35-4-233. **USC**-Leinart 20-31-0-231.

Receiving: **Colorado State**-Anderson 9-137; Dreessen 5-23; Walker 4-66; Jaunarajs 1-7. **USC**-Smith 8-79; McFoy 4-59; Jarrett 3-32; Kirtman 2-30; White 1-22; Holmes 1-7; Bush 1-2.

Individual Defensive Statistics
Interceptions: **Colorado State**-None. **USC**-Grootegoed 2-57; Wright 1-0; Sartz 1-8.

Sacks: **Colorado State**-None. **USC**-Cody 1; Patterson 1; Wright 1; Schweiger 1.

Tackles (Unassisted-Assisted): **Colorado State**-Kochevar 5-3; Jones 5-2; Stratton 4-3; Hall 4-3; Cathy 3-3; Herbert 3-1; Simon 2-2; Goodpaster 2-2; Adkins 3-0; Garcia 2-1; Witt 2-1; M. Vomhof 1-2. **USC**-Wright 3-3; Tatupu 2-4; Leach 5-0; Nunn 1-4; Rivers 1-4; Schweiger 2-2; Cody 2-2; Ashton 0-4; Wyatt 2-1; Ware 1-2; Jackson 0-3.

"It was good to hear some of the seniors who have been here a long time and how much work they put in," he said.

Freshman center Jeff Byers, the Gatorade National Player of the Year, played all but two series in the second half and also got the message.

ABOVE: LenDale White dives into the end zone for the first score of the game. *Staff photo by Evan Yee*

"We're playing for ourselves," he said. "That's what matters. There's the fans and our families, but in the end, we have to play for ourselves."

Maybe Colorado State (0-2) regretted working so hard to schedule the game last fall, although the Rams might not have fared much better against surging Fresno State, the team they canceled from their schedule. "We bit off more than you could chew, you could say," Colorado State coach Sonny Lubick said.

It didn't quite look that way early. The Rams trailed 7-0 but drove to USC's 15-yard line when quarterback Justin Holland's pass was intercepted by Grootegoed, who returned it 57 yards and set up the Trojans' second touchdown.

"I tried to bail out the defense," Grootegoed said.

Carroll was more effusive, especially since he's also the defensive coordinator.

"He decoyed very well on a route he knew was coming and for him to come away with

two interceptions on the day is just awesome, especially for a linebacker," Carroll said.

The offense also made strides, including the youthful receivers. Even freshman Dwayne Jarrett rebounded with a high-reaching touchdown catch with three defenders surrounding him. That almost made up for the four passes he dropped.

"We were going to just keep feeding him the ball," Carroll said. "We know what he can do in practice."

Leinart also praised the young receivers, who helped give him jitters against Virginia Tech by running the wrong routes.

"It's funny how everyone acts like they're struggling," he said. "Yeah, the timing was off in Virginia Tech but it was our first game. I'm proud of the way they've improved."

It's doubtful a players-only meeting will be called this week.

"We weren't where we wanted to be the last game," tight end Alex Holmes said. "Today, we played the way we think we should."

RIGHT: Dwayne Jarrett leaps to catch a touchdown pass. *Staff photo by Evan Yee*

USC Leaves BYU Gasping in Thin Ai

BY SCOTT WOLF, *STAFF WRITER*

PROVO, Utah—At its best, USC can make a crowd breathless. The top-ranked Trojans were far from it Saturday night, but in faltering they revealed a side almost more dangerous.

USC provided only five or six true moments of its potential, but those devastated the crowd and, ultimately, BYU during a 42-10 victory in front of 63,467 at LaVell Edwards Stadium. It didn't look easy, unless you consider the highlight reel plays, which accounted for the victory. Most were provided by tailback Reggie Bush, who gained 124 yards and scored two touchdowns.

"Obviously, it's a relief when you have those plays," Bush said. "Big-play offense, that's what we play for."

But even as Bush drew attention, tailback LenDale White reeled off a 43-yard run in the fourth quarter to give the Trojans a 35-10 advantage. That pushed White over the 100-yard barrier and gave USC two 100-yard rushers in a game for the first time since 1996, when Chad Morton and LaVale Woods did it against Oregon State.

That stat would seem esoteric in the first half, when the Trojans appeared in danger of losing. Just when it looked like USC's 11-game winning streak would end, the Trojans scored three touchdowns in the final eight minutes of the first half to take a comfortable 21-3 lead.

"This is not an unusual type game for us," USC coach Pete Carroll said. "I don't ever allow our team or coaches to pass judgment in the first quarter."

The Trojans turned the game around in the second quarter. Bush caught a 21-yard pass from quarterback Matt Leinart and then broke a 66-yard run for USC's first two touchdowns, and wide receiver Dwayne Jarrett caught a 15-yard touchdown pass to erase BYU's 3-0 lead.

It quickly silenced an increasingly noisy crowd that sensed the possibility of an upset.

Although Leinart is the official Heisman Trophy candidate, Bush once again wowed a national television audience watching on ESPN, like he did three weeks ago against Virginia Tech.

The tailback juked past five tacklers on his way after catching a 21-yard touchdown pass from Leinart that was actually more a run.

"We started off shaky, but the second quarter turned things around," Bush said.

The touchdown came just as BYU's crowd started to reach a near-deafening level and quickly quieted the fans as the Trojans took a 7-3 lead with 8:30 left in the half.

It was a later-than-usual first score for the Trojans, who were shut out in the first quarter for the first time since 2002 against Notre Dame.

Then, USC (3-0) broke the game open.

Bush took an anything-but-unusual handoff and went toward the line, then broke through and sped past the defense en route to a 66-yard score.

"He jogged the last 40 yards," Carroll said.

LEFT: Matt Leinart threw two touchdown passes and ran for one as USC beat BYU. *George Frey/Getty Images*

	1	2	3	4	Score
USC	0	21	0	21	42
Brigham Young	0	3	7	0	10

Scoring Summary

BYU - Payne 46-yard field goal, 10 plays, 48 yards in 3:39
USC - Bush 21-yard pass from Leinart (Killeen kick), eight plays, 60 yards in 2:00
USC - Bush 66-yard run (Killeen kick), two plays, 73 yards in 0:18
USC - Jarrett 15-yard pass from Leinart (Killeen kick), three plays, 20 yards in 0:53
BYU - Watkins 69-yard pass from Beck (Payne kick), one play, 69 yards in 0:11
USC - Leinart 1-yard run (Killeen kick), 10 plays, 71 yards in 2:54
USC - White 43-yard run (Killeen kick), four plays, 71 yards in 0:48
USC - Webb 9-yard run (Killeen kick), 11 plays, 43 yards in 6:42

Team Statistics

	USC	BYU
First Downs	26	11
Rushes-Yards (Net)	50-291	24-27
Passing Yards (Net)	236	194
Passes Att-Comp-Int	35-22-1	34-18-3
Total Offense Plays-Yards	85-527	58-221
Punt Returns-Yards	2-7	1-0
Kickoff Returns-Yards	1-38	1-26
Punts (Number-Avg)	4-44.0	8-48.2
Fumbles-Lost	0-0	3-1
Penalties-Yards	8-73	7-54
Possession Time	36:45	23:02
Third-Down Conversions	12 of 19	4 of 15
Fourth-Down Conversions	1 of 1	0 of 0
Sacks by (Number-Yards):	3-27	2-17

Individual Offensive Statistics

Rushing: USC-Bush 14-124; White 17-110; Reed 7-21; Dennis 3-18; Leinart 7-10; Webb 1-9; Team 1-(-1).
Brigham Young-Tahi 7-27; Brown 6-15; Hudson 1-1; Collie 2-(-3); Beck 8-(-13).

Passing: USC-Leinart 22-35-1-236.
Brigham Young-Beck 18-34-3-194.

Receiving: USC-Smith 6-62; Bush 4-42; McFoy 4-37; Jarrett 3-58; Kirtman 2-19; Holmes 2-11; White 1-7.
Brigham Young-Watkins 4-94; Collie 4-36; Coats 3-25; Tahi 3-10; Brown 2-8; Wilkerson 1-14; Kukahiko 1-7.

Individual Defensive Statistics

Interceptions: USC-Bing 1-8; Thomas 1-29; Grootegoed 1-0.
Brigham Young-Burbidge 1-23.

Sacks (Unassisted-Assisted): USC-Cody 2-0; Schweiger 1-0.
Brigham Young-White 1-0; Poppinga 1-0.

Tackles (Unassisted-Assisted): USC-Tatupu 2-5; Leach 5-0; Grootegoed 3-1; Ashton 3-1; Bing 1-3; Cody 3-0; Wyatt 2-1; Rucker 2-0; Thomas 2-0; Wright 2-0.
Brigham Young-Francisco 8-8; Burbidge 7-4; Heaney 4-6; Soelberg 5-4; Jensen 2-6; White 2-5; Poppinga 1-4; Denney 0-5; Brown 2-2; Buchanan 2-0; Paongo 2-0.

To make matters worse for the Cougars, quarterback John Beck fumbled the snap on the next play, and Lofa Tatupu recovered at the BYU 20-yard line.

Leinart found Jarrett open in the end zone for a 21-3 lead with 1:05 left in the half.

Just like that, the Trojans were back in their usual commanding position.

"This was a really cool momentum change," Carroll said. "Sometimes, we don't start real fast. We just had to be patient. They got shots defensively, but if you're patient, you'll get your shots in, too."

Prior to that, the Trojans barely resembled the No. 1 team in the nation.

Leinart got off to an unlikely start as he underthrew Steve Smith and was intercepted by safety Jon Burbidge. It was Leinart's first interception in 111 attempts and first of the season. He threw three interceptions last season against BYU.

BELOW: Pete Carroll argues a call in a game that saw the No. 1 ranked Trojans pull away in the fourth quarter.
George Frey/Getty Images

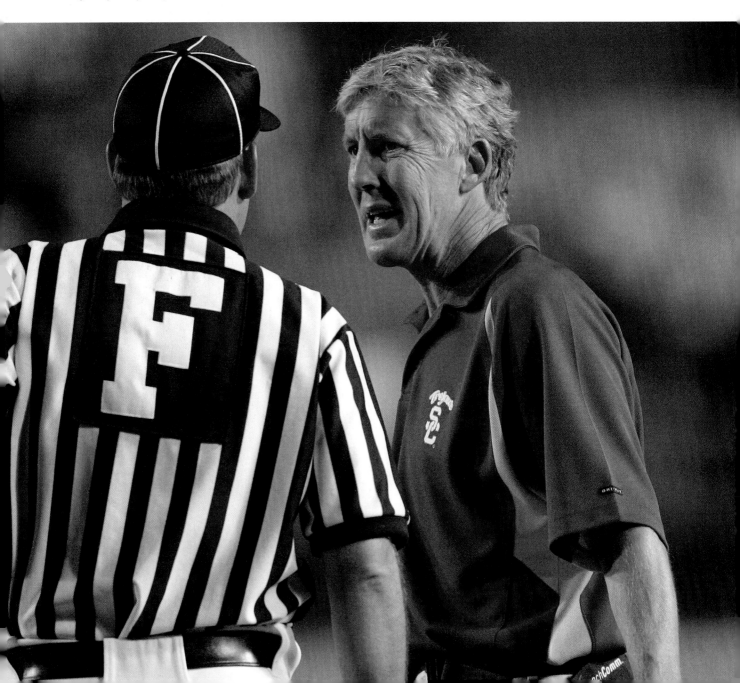

ABOVE: Shaun Cody (84) records one of his two sacks. *George Frey/Getty Images*

#5 REGGIE BUSH

BY KEVIN MODESTI, STAFF WRITER

From the kickoff to the final tick of the Rose Bowl clock in the 74th USC-UCLA football game Saturday afternoon, Reggie Bush did whatever was superhumanly possible—cutting, spinning, even somersaulting—to avoid the grasp of larger men.

Then, with the 29-24 victory by top-ranked USC over a tough rival in the books, Bush had a change of heart. Sprinting to the Trojans' rooting section behind the north goal posts, the kid who'd just racked up 335 total yards glad-handed his way through family and friends and into the arms of a bearded presence wearing a cardinal jersey with a gold No. 5 and the name Dad.

"He told me he loves me and it was a great game," Reggie said after the embrace with Lamar Bush of San Diego.

Lamar came away from the hug talking proudly of his 19-year-old son, reborn as a Heisman Trophy contender on the last day of the Trojans' perfect regular season in a game in which he rushed for 204 yards and two long touchdowns, caught passes for 73 yards, and returned kicks and punts for 58.

"Of course, I think he deserves it," the elder Bush said of the Heisman, grinning at his obvious bias. "He doesn't really talk about it. If he wins it, he wins it. He just wants to go to the ceremony. He's never been to New York."

Give that young man an airline ticket.

While we're at it, give him the Heisman.

Let's hope the voters were watching the UCLA game as the most exciting player in the game showed all of his talents (right down to his gift for the ill-timed fumble).

Reggie Bush comes at defenses such as UCLA's with runs shaped like a question mark. He'll slide one way, cut back the other way, then make a straight line for the end zone. His 2,181 all-purpose yards this season, the most by a Trojan since Marcus Allen's 2,683 as the 1981 Heisman winner, don't include the hundreds he covers from side to side.

Today, the question mark punctuates the final argument for Bush's Heisman candidacy.

"Why not?"

The national consensus, after the Trojans' rout of Notre Dame last week, was that Matt Leinart's five touchdown passes had made the USC quarterback the front-runner for college football's top individual honor. The Web site heismanprojection.com, sort of an exit poll for balloting that closes Wednesday, had Leinart on top this week, followed by Oklahoma running back Adrian Peterson and quarterback Jason White, and Utah quarterback Alex Smith. Then came Bush.

An espn.com "experts" poll made it Leinart ahead of Peterson, White, Smith, Texas running back Cedric Benson and Cal quarterback Aaron Rodgers. Then Bush.

"I think I shook loose some Heisman votes (against UCLA)," Bush said as darkness fell on the Rose Bowl.

He thinks he has "as good a chance as anybody" but really doesn't expect to win the trophy, which will be awarded next Saturday in Manhattan in a televised ceremony attended by however many top vote-getters are invited. He's only a sophomore, notes the six-foot tailback from San Diego's Helix High. Besides, he expressed surprise when the Pacific-10 Conference made him its co-player of the year with Leinart.

"He and Matt are friends," said Lamar Bush, who walked out of the stadium with an orange in his right hand, a symbol of USC's all-but-official berth in the Jan. 4 Orange Bowl game for the national championship. "If Matt wins, he'd be real happy."

Leinart is even more magnanimous, saying Bush should get the Heisman.

"He's the best player in college football," Leinart said after failing to throw a touchdown pass for the first time in 26 starts at USC. "He's like (former Trojans wide receiver) Mike Williams—he can change the game with one touch of the ball."

Class: *Sophomore*
Hometown: *Spring Valley, California*
High School: *Helix*
Major: *Psychology*
Position: *Tailback*
Height: *6'0"*
Weight: *200*

Staff photo by Michael Owen Baker

Bush got 25 touches and averaged 13.4 yards Saturday as the Trojans beat the Bruins for the sixth year in a row. His 204 yards rushing were the most by a Trojan since Shawn Walters' 234 against Stanford early in the 1994 season. Faking out linebacker Justin London and cornerback Trey Brown and outrunning corner Matt Clark in the second quarter, he completed an 81-yard touchdown run that was the longest by a Trojan since LaVale Woods' 96-yarder against Oregon State in 1996.

That was his less spectacular run on this chilly afternoon. On the game's second play from scrimmage, Bush started right, cut left and beat safety Ben Emanuel and finally Clark. Hearing footsteps, Bush launched himself over the goal line and ended up somersaulting into the end zone. He was flagged for a debatable unsportsman-like-conduct penalty.

The highlight-reel play may have relaunched his Heisman bid.

"This is my first time. I don't know what you have to do to win a Heisman," Bush said. "I just want to go (to New York) and enjoy the experience. I love to travel. I love to shop for clothes and shoes. I hear they have some nice stores there."

Half-Cooked

BY SCOTT WOLF, *STAFF WRITER*

STANFORD, Calif.—As he walked off the field at halftime, USC coach Pete Carroll knew Stanford's Buddy Teevens out-coached him. At least that's what he was told by the screaming fans.

"Those guys in the tunnel thought so," Carroll said. "I sure heard them at halftime. I turned to someone and said, 'This is just like New England.'"

Actually, it wasn't quite like coaching the New England Patriots, because as Carroll emerged from the locker room after the game, a fan yelled, "Great job."

And it also wasn't New England because top-ranked USC overcame an at times awful first-half performance to defeat the Cardinal 31-28 in front of 55,750 at Stanford Stadium.

It was perhaps the most dramatic victory of the Carroll era, because it included a rare fourth-quarter comeback, which was necessary because of the 28-17 halftime deficit.

"We were reeling in the first half," Carroll said.

That was an understatement. Everything that went wrong could be illustrated by the final play of the half, as Stanford attempted to run out the clock.

Tom Hauck/Icon SMI

In what should be one of the strangest plays of the season, tailback J.R. Lemon took a simple handoff, broke through the line and caught most of USC's defense asleep, racing 82 yards for a touchdown as time expired.

"We were thinking about our halftime speeches," defensive tackle Shaun Cody said. "We were in a funky defense. I didn't know what was going on."

The play electrified the crowd and could have dealt a knockout blow to the Trojans, who hadn't trailed a game by more than 10 points since last season's lone loss to California.

Instead it managed to ignite USC (4-0) and brought forth a flurry of halftime speeches from players. So much so that Carroll barely needed to speak.

"That touchdown wasn't deflating at all. It got us upset," linebacker Matt Grootegoed said. "As soon as that happened, that was the turning point."

Offensive lineman John Drake and Fred Matua, along with Cody and defensive end Frostee Rucker, took turns in the locker room making sure USC got its act together.

"I thought we were going to get cussed out by the coaches," Rucker said. "Usually only a couple of people feel it at halftime but this time it was the whole team. We didn't need Coach Carroll and the coaches to yell at us."

Drake said the main message was the offensive and defensive lines would dominate the second half.

"Stanford's not Sister Mary of the Blind," Drake said. "They beat the same team we beat (Brigham Young). They came out with jabs but this was a 12-round fight."

Quarterback Matt Leinart, who didn't speak, said he also felt relaxed despite being down 11 points.

LEFT: Matt Leinart threw for 284 yards and ran for a touchdown, helping the Trojans erase an 11-point deficit and defeat the Cardinal, 31-28.
David Gonazales/Icon SMI

	1	2	3	4	Score
USC	10	7	7	7	31
Stanford	7	21	0	0	28

Scoring Summary
USC - Killeen 23-yard field goal, 11 plays, 69 yards in 4:20
USC - Smith 2-yard pass from Leinart (Killeen), one play, two yards in 0:04
STAN - Moore 3-yard pass from Edwards (Sgroi kick), 11 plays, 79 yards in 4:51
STAN - Danahy 2-yard pass from Edwards (Sgroi kick), 15 plays, 76 yards in 7:26
STAN - Matter 11-yard run (Sgroi kick), seven plays, 33 yards in 2:50
USC - Bush 17-yard run (Killeen kick), six plays, 66 yards in 2:08
STAN - Lemon 82-yard run (Sgroi kick), two plays, 80 yards in 0:52
USC - Leinart 1-yard run (Killeen kick), four plays, 63 yards in 1:34
USC - White 2-yard run (Killeen kick), eight plays, 41 yards in 3:06

Team Statistics
	USC	STAN
First Downs	23	17
Rushes-Yards (Net)	34-99	30-144
Passing Yds (Net)	308	183
Passes Att-Comp-Int	30-23-1	35-23-1
Total Offense Plays-Yards	64-383	65-327
Punt Returns-Yards	3-40	3-22
Kickoff Returns-Yards	4-85	5-147
Punts (Number-Avg)	3-40.3	5-42.4
Fumbles-Lost	3-1	3-0
Penalties-Yards	2-20	6-35
Possession Time	29:01	30:59
Sacks By (Number-Yards)	3-28	2-19

Individual Offensive Statistics
Rushing: **USC**-Bush 16-95; White 11-24; Dennis 1-1; Team 2-(- 5); Leinart 4-(-16).
Stanford-Lemon 10-96; Tolon 9-26; Matter 1-11; Edwards 10-11.

Passing: **USC**-Leinart 23-30-1-284.
Stanford-Edwards 23-35-1-183.

Receiving: **USC**-Smith 7-129; Jarrett 5-54; Bush 4-25; Holmes 2-29; McFoy 2-28; Kirtman 2-4; Davis 1-15.
Stanford-Moore 5-47; Smith 5-45; McCullum 5-36; Bradford 4-30; Marrero 3-23; Danahy 1-2.

Individual Defensive Statistics
Interceptions: **USC**-Arbet, Kevin 1-66.
Stanford-Silva, Mike 1-0.

Sacks (Unassisted-Assisted): **USC**-Rivers 2-0; Jackson 1-0.
Stanford-Silva 1-0; Carroll 1-0.

Tackles (Unassisted-Assisted): **USC**-Tatupu 7-3; Grootegoed 5-2; Leach 5-1; Bing 5-1; Nunn 3-1; Sartz 1-3; Rivers 3-0; Arbet 3-0; Cody 3-0; Patterson 2-0; Jackson 2-0.
Stanford-Schimmelmann 7-3; Rushing 7-1; Alston 4-4; Atogwe 3-4; Harrison 4-2; Wilson 4-0; Scharff 1-3; Jenkins 3-0; Torrence 2-1; Silva 2-1; Oshinowo 2-1.

"I just had a smile on my face. It was fun," he said. "We haven't had too many close games."

Whatever happened, it worked because the defense completely shut down the Cardinal.

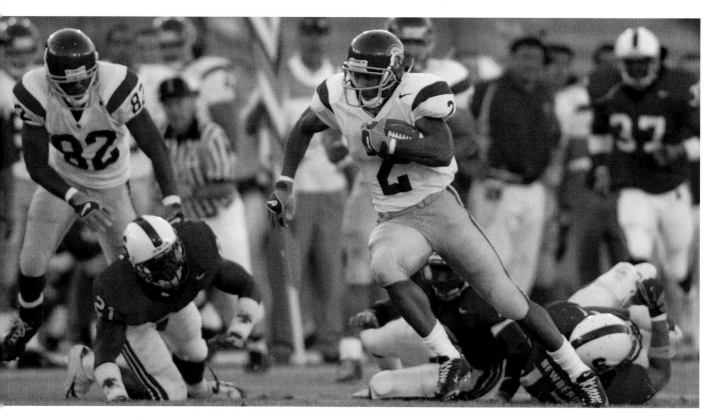

ABOVE: Steve Smith (2) paced the USC receivers with seven catches and 129 yards. *Tom Hauck/Icon SMI*

In a complete reverse of the first half, Stanford barely had the ball in the second. The Trojans' defense held the Cardinal to 36 yards offense and kept four of the five drives to under five yards.

And the offense did just enough to win. Although Leinart completed 24 of 30 passes for 308 yards, this still was a nail-biter. He completed a 51-yard pass to Steve Smith to set up the first touchdown, his own one-yard run with 3:06 left in the third quarter to make it 28-24.

But kicker Ryan Killeen missed a 23-yard field goal with 11 minutes left that could have robbed the Trojans' momentum.

"That ticked me off," Smith said. "It took a little bit out of us."

Stanford (2-1) gained just four yards on its next possession, and after an incredible 33-yard punt return from Reggie Bush in which he broke four tackles, the Trojans needed to go just 41 yards for the winning touchdown.

LenDale White, nursing an aggravated ankle sprain, scored on a 2-yard run with 6:15 left to give USC its 31-28 victory.

"Coach Carroll came up and asked if I could get it in and I told him I'd get it in," White said.

By the end of the game, USC retained its undefeated season by a slim margin, and it was almost as if the first half never happened.

"I know people wonder how you have games like this," Carroll said.

"It ain't going to be easy. It's hard to do this week after week."

He added: "Our guys at halftime wouldn't accept it. In their young minds, there was no doubt. The coach might have some."

One key final question: Were they Stanford or USC fans yelling at Carroll at halftime?

"I don't know," he said. "But I'd heard it before."

BELOW: LenDale White scored the final touchdown, giving USC its three-point margin of victory.
Tom Hauck/Icon SMI

Anything but Bear Market for This Game

BY SCOTT WOLF, *STAFF WRITER*

Mike Williams doesn't play for USC anymore, he just remains the Trojans' best spokesman.

"If we win three games this year, they will be against Cal, UCLA and Notre Dame," the former receiver said. "Actually we've already won three games this year, but those will be three more we will win."

Cal mentioned in the same breath as archrivals Notre Dame and UCLA? Williams' comments illustrate just how important the Golden Bears have become to top-ranked USC.

Seventh-ranked Cal was the last team to defeat USC, a span of 13 games, and this week's matchup at the Coliseum is a sellout and drawing national attention, with the appearance of ESPN's "GameDay" college football show.

"It's like state bragging rights," USC offensive lineman John Drake said. "It gives a little more juice to the season. Everyone's circled the Cal game."

For an added indication of how important Saturday's game will be, Williams intends to make his first appearance of the season.

"I'm going to be there on the sideline," he said.

"I'll make it and talk to the dudes. It's a big deal. I don't think there will be a lot of revenge talk. But it will be in the back of our minds."

USC defensive lineman Shaun Cody said he hasn't thought much about last season's 34-31 triple-overtime loss, unless he runs into fans.

"I just hear it all the time, people come up and say, "You guys could have won,'" Cody said. "It's been a while since we played them but I definitely remember that feeling (from losing). I definitely think it's become a rivalry again. It's fun to have that. They're good and we're good."

Losing to Cal last year was an unusual feeling for the Trojans, the only setback over the past 25 games, but the manner of the loss also was unique, according to Williams.

"That was one of the few games we made second-half adjustments and a team was still able to put points on the board against us," Williams said.

Actually, Cal scored just three points in the second half, before outscoring USC 10-7 in overtime.

Cody remembers Cal exploiting USC's defensive line, which frequently shifted positions before the snap during the first half, when the Bears took a 21-7 lead.

The Trojans were more effective after going to their base defense in the second half.

"We're not worried too much about blitzing," he said. "We usually run our base stuff."

Staff photo by John McCoy

"It doesn't have any bearing on us unless we allow it to. I'm tense for all the games. There isn't a game we play that doesn't mean everything to me."

—USC Coach Pete Carroll

But Williams thinks this year's game is different, because the Trojans already made a second-half comeback against Stanford and know what it's like to overcome a slow start.

"Guys understand how to step it up. Last year, Cal was the first time being down. We didn't have that experience yet," Williams said. "It goes without saying the nucleus of this team are the guys who lost to Cal."

USC coach Pete Carroll doesn't like to make any game more important than another, but he's keenly aware of the extra hype this week, and sometimes tries to use it for motivational purposes.

"It doesn't have any bearing on us unless we allow it to," Carroll said. "I'm tense for all the games. There isn't a game we play that doesn't mean everything to me."

Even Drake said the idea that USC sat around and waited a year to avenge last year's loss to Cal is overrated.

"I don't lose any sleep over it, but I wouldn't mind trading it away," he said. "I don't know if it bothers me, but perfection is what we shoot for."

Trojans Avoid Another Upset

BY SCOTT WOLF, *STAFF WRITER*

Nine yards and 90,000 screaming fans were all that stood between USC and ruin Saturday, as the Trojans nearly threw away their No. 1 ranking as well as their conference and national title hopes.

It was enough to bring USC quarterback Matt Leinart to a knee. "I was just praying," he said.

Fortunately for USC, its strong-willed seniors did more than pray in the defensive huddle, with Cal poised to score the game-winning touchdown, first-and-goal at the 9-yard line with 1:47 remaining.

"I said it's nine yards to the Pac-10 championship," defensive tackle Shaun Cody said. "In the heat of the game, you don't always realize it, but sometimes, you think about that stuff."

The defense, exhausted from being on the field far too long, listened to Cody and stopped Cal to preserve a 23-17 victory over the seventh-ranked Golden Bears.

"We used the crowd there for energy," linebacker Matt Grootegoed said. "My ankle was killing me."

Defensive end Frostee Rucker added, "I was exhausted, but the scene was set. The seniors told us that it was their last nine yards against Cal."

The memorable conclusion kept USC (5-0, 2-0) undefeated and almost obscured the fact that the Trojans were outplayed for most of the game.

A marvelous performance from Cal quarterback Aaron Rodgers, who completed his first 23 passes and finished 29 of 34 for 267 yards and one touchdown, wasn't quite enough at the finish.

Rodgers' 23 consecutive completions tied an NCAA record set by Tennessee's Tee Martin in 1998, and his 26 in a row over two games broke Martin's NCAA record for consecutive completions in a season.

USC coach Pete Carroll was unaware Rodgers completed 23 consecutive passes.

"There would be too much pain if I knew that," Carroll said. "It was frustrating. They were satisfied to dink the football. We had to wait it out. They were really happy to get five yards."

And why not? The Bears and their coach, Jeff Tedford, were on the verge of their second victory over USC in 15 games, the only team to defeat the Trojans in the past 26 contests.

Instead, USC ran its winning streak to 14 in a row despite an anemic offensive performance as Leinart endured his shakiest effort of the season, completing 15 of 25 passes for 164 yards, two touchdowns and an interception.

It didn't help that leading receiver Steve Smith broke his left leg early in the third quarter, or that the running game disappeared.

If Cal (3-1, 1-1) scored on its final possession, USC offensive coordinator Norm Chow knew who would be blamed.

"I think we would have taken all the heat," Chow said. "We didn't do our part."

LEFT: Dwayne Jarrett is upended after a catch in the first quarter. *Staff photo by John McCoy*

	1	2	3	4	Score
California	0	10	7	0	17
USC	10	6	7	0	23

Scoring Summary
USC - White 5-yard pass from Leinart (Killeen kick), nine plays, 31 yards in 4:32
USC - Killeen 31-yard field goal, seven plays, 50 yards in 2:28
CAL - Schneider 39-yard field goal, 12 plays, 58 yards in 4:48
USC - Killeen 33-yard field goal, four plays, one yard in 0:53
CAL - McArthur 20-yard pass from Rodgers (Schneider kick), nine plays, 80 yards in 4:40
USC - Killeen 42-yard field goal, nine plays, 37 yards in 1:34
USC - Jarrett 16-yard pass from Leinart (Killeen kick), seven plays, 66 yards in 2:49
CAL - Lynch 2-yard run (Schneider kick), 12 plays, 80 yards in 6:41

Team Statistics

	CAL	USC
First Downs	28	12
Rushes-Yards (Net)	44-157	25-41
Passing Yards (Net)	267	164
Passes Att-Comp-Int	35-29-0	25-15-1
Total Offense Plays-Yards	79-424	50-205
Punt Returns-Yards	2-6	0-0
Kickoff Returns-Yards	0-0	4-124
Punts (Number-Avg)	0-0.0	2-57.0
Fumbles-Lost.	4-3	1-0
Penalties-Yards	6-46	5-36
Possession Time	37:11	22:49
Sacks by (Number-Yards)	4-30	5-20

Individual Offensive Statistics
Rushing: **California**-Arrington 21-112; Lynch 8-36; Manderino 3-15; Rodgers 10-7; Team 2-(-13).
USC-White 11-52; Bush 8-23; Team 2-(-4); Leinart 4-(-30).

Passing: **California**-Rodgers 29-34-0-267; Lyman 0-1-0-0.
USC-Leinart 15-24-1-164; Team 0-1-0-0.

Receiving: **California**-McArthur 7-101; Cross 5-40;Arrington 4-26; Toler 3-16; Lynch 3-9; Lyman 2-28; Makonnen 2-22; Manderino 2-21; Smith 1-4.
USC-Jarrett 4-37; Smith 2-76; McFoy 2-20; White 2-10; Holmes 2-8; Bush 1-6; Mitchell 1-5; Kirtman 1-2.

Individual Defensive Statistics
Interceptions: **California**-Smith 1-13.
USC-None.

Sacks (Unassisted-Assisted): **California**-Mebane 1-1; Riddle 1-1; Hunter 1-0.
USC-Jackson 1-1; Wright 1-0; Cody 1-0; Rucker 0-1; Patterson 1-0.

Tackles (Unassisted-Assisted): **California**-Hunter 8-1; Riddle 5-1; Mixon 5-1; Gutierrez 3-1; Blay-Miezah 2-2; Smith 1-2; Team 2-0; Foltz 2-0; Hughes 2-0.
USC-Tatupu 4-9; Ware 8-4; Patterson 7-3; Sartz 4-6; Arbet 4-3; Rucker 3-3; Grootegoed 3-3; E. Wright 3-2; Wyatt 4-0; Leach 2-2; Cody 2-2; Team 3-0; N. Wright 2-1.

The Trojans barely even had the ball, with Cal's offense on the field for more than 37 minutes, compared to USC, which had the ball for fewer than 23. The Bears totaled 424 yards in

ABOVE: USC defenders celebrate in the endzone after deflecting a fourth-quarter pass, sealing the Trojan victory. *Staff photo by John McCoy*

offense; USC totaled just 205, its fewest yards in a victory since 1986.

"I think we ran an all-time low number of plays," Chow said.

USC's 50 plays were its fewest since getting 49 against Texas Christian in the 1998 Sun Bowl.

And yet, the Trojans won. Even though Cal moved the ball, it was hurt by turnovers. A bobbled snap on the game's first punt led to USC's first touchdown. A fumbled punt return directly led to a USC field goal.

"I feel we could beat these guys nine times out of 10," Cal free safety Ryan Gutierrez said. "This just happened to be the one day."

Even with Cal's three fumbles, the Bears trailed 23-17 entering the fourth quarter and staged two impressive drives. The first one ended with kicker Tom Schneider missing a 36-yard field goal.

The second drive saw the Bears with a first-and-goal situation at USC's 9. Carroll, USC's defensive coordinator, admitted he wanted his unit to settle the game.

"My sick way of looking at this, and I've often been in this situation, is that this is the best it can get," Carroll said. "I tried to convey it to the players and they thought it was crazy."

Rodgers threw an incomplete pass to Noah Smith (Taft of Woodland Hills) on first down, then was sacked by Manuel Wright for a five-yard loss.

Cal's best chance to score came on third down, when Rodgers fired a pass at wide receiver Geoff McArthur in the end zone. Carroll thought McArthur had a touchdown, but cornerback Eric Wright dove and broke McArthur's concentration.

"The DB put his hand out at the last minute, it distracted me," McArthur said. "I should have made the catch."

On fourth down, USC rushed four linemen, and Rodgers scrambled before throwing an

incomplete pass to Jonathan Makonnen with cornerback Kevin Arbet tightly covering him.

A livid Tedford walked 15 yards on to the field, claiming pass interference.

"I'm not sure if (Makonnen) slipped or got hooked," Tedford said.

In an unusual postgame exchange, the players from both teams calmly walked off exchanging feelings of respect, a sign of the burgeoning rivalry.

"It was total exhaustion," Rucker said. "Just handshakes and hugs."

"I hadn't played in a game of this caliber," McArthur said. "Unbelievable, in front of all these people."

BELOW: Reggie Bush fumbled a kickoff, then recovered the ball to move deep into Cal territory in the third quarter.
Staff photo by John McCoy

PETE CARROLL

BY STEVE DILBECK, *STAFF WRITER*

Forget about it. Close the door. Push it so far away it can't even be heard from again. Pete Carroll, you've found your calling. You've found your place in the universe. A place precious few will ever know. All that tradition, all those expectations and pressure and scrutiny, and you've turned USC into your place. Your home.

A home where something amazing has happened, and, in truth, it could be only the beginning.

A marvelous amalgamation of enthusiasm, experience, knowledge and innate football sense have fashioned you into the best college football coach in the land.

At this place, at this time.

Embrace it for that true rarity it is. In just two years, you transformed USC into a Pete Carroll lovefest. Players, recruits, administrators, alumni, media—they all love you.

They're all caught up in the Carroll Express, and there's no reason to stop now or in the foreseeable future.

Sure, the NFL is still out there. Still intriguing. The place you spent 16 years of your life. Still offering the best football and highest paychecks in America.

So naturally the suspicion—or fear—remains you will get bored with all this college success, look for a new challenge and return to the NFL to conquer a world that previously slipped your grasp. Banish the thought from your mind. Exile it to the deepest portion of your cerebrum.

"I don't see getting bored," Carroll said. "I think the challenge of maintaining is what always keeps me going and will always keep me going. It's the challenge of how long can you keep it going at a high level.

"I don't know what that means, or how many that means, or games or seasons or any of that stuff, but that's what I'm charged up about."

You won one national title last season and are currently ranked No. 1 and on track to play in the BCS title game for a second consecutive championship.

Consecutive national championships has happened once since 1979. It's an extraordinary accomplishment, manufactured in an extraordinary time period.

Steve Spurrier signed a five-year, $25 million contract when he left Florida for the Washington Redskins. Two years later, the toast of the SEC had enough. Now he works on his golf game.

You've said before it's not about the money, and even if people believe you, there's this undeniable sense that your returning to the NFL is inevitable, that it's simply a matter of time.

That conquering the college world year after year will lose its allure. That the fire within you, that burns so bright you look almost searing to the touch, will dim and you'll seek a new challenge.

"If I ever get used to winning at this kind of level, and I'm willing to throw that away, you can drag me out and leave me on the beach somewhere," Carroll said.

"I may just quit coaching. Because the opportunity to win and to maintain a high level of success is so clearly in front of us here. It's more important than anything else to me in the coaching world.

"As far as losing interest, I'm captivated by what I'm doing."

And there is no reason to believe things have ebbed. Top recruiting class follows top recruiting class. Kids want to play for you, for someone so energetic, so willing to make everyone feel part of the team, so willing to play freshmen and seniors alike.

> **Birthdate:** *September 15, 1951*
> **Hometown:** *San Francisco, California*
> **Position:** *Head Coach*
> **Career Record:** *42-9*
> **Record at USC:** *42-9, two national championships*

You could walk away from this?

"I don't want that," said sophomore receiver Steve Smith. "I want him to stay. I know it's a possibility, but I don't think it's going to happen.

No Doubt in Rout

BY SCOTT WOLF, *STAFF WRITER*

f USC didn't enter the Coliseum for free Saturday, the Trojans themselves might have asked for a refund.

It's not that top-ranked USC didn't appreciate a blowout, especially after narrow victories over Stanford and California, but a 45-7 rout of Arizona State even left the Trojans wanting.

"I thought it was going to be closer," USC wide receiver Chris McFoy said. "Cal was just better. A lot better. Arizona State seemed like they were scared. The quarterback looked scared."

Tailback LenDale White admitted he didn't care how many points USC wins by, but this was hardly four-star entertainment for the masses, especially for the announced 90,211 in attendance.

"If I could pick a game, I'd rather be in the Cal game," White said.

Not everyone is a critic, though, and defensive tackle Shaun Cody appreciated this game, or half-game, which is how long it took the Trojans to embarrass the 15th-ranked Sun Devils.

"It's a lot of fun to have a close game, but it's tough on the heart," Cody said. "Today we wanted to make a statement. We definitely think we haven't shown a complete game, and this was the first case."

USC (6-0, 3-0 Pacific-10 Conference) dominated easily enough to virtually guarantee being atop the first Bowl Championship Series rankings. More importantly, the lopsided score allowed some rare trash talking directed at who else? ESPN.

"Is Mark May here? Kirk Herbstreit?" said USC coach Pete Carroll, referring to the cable network's analysts.

"On ESPN, they said Arizona State would win," defensive tackle Manuel Wright said. "We keep putting up Ws. They can't say anything."

Glad to see everyone's priorities are in order. But USC was probably thinking about ESPN the whole second half because there wasn't anything else to do. The Trojans led 42-7 at halftime, and it was hard to tell if they were that good or Arizona State was that bad.

Who could explain why quarterback Andrew Walter threw to a receiver who wasn't double- or triple-covered, but quadruple-covered? Predictably, linebacker Matt Grootegoed easily intercepted the pass.

This is the same quarterback who entered the game with 15 touchdown passes and only one interception. Arizona State allowed just eight sacks in its first five games. Walter was sacked six times Saturday.

"He can't run," Wright said. "They can't throw, and they only have one running back. They were a one-dimensional team."

Who would expect the Sun Devils cornerbacks to refuse to turn and look for the ball on pass plays, or single-cover wide receiver Dwayne Jarrett (five receptions, 139 yards) despite repeatedly burned for big plays?

LEFT: Lofa Tatupu (58) sacks ASU quarterback Andew Walter during the first half of the 45-7 rout.
Staff photo by Hans Gutknecht

	1	2	3	4	Score
Arizona State	0	7	0	0	7
USC	14	28	0	3	45

Scoring Summary

USC - Bush 10-yard pass from Leinart (Killeen kick), eight plays, 45 yards in 3:27

USC - White 9-yard pass from Leinart (Killeen kick), seven plays, 50 yards in 3:56

USC - Jarrett 19-yard pass from Leinart (Killeen kick), one play, 19 yards in 0:05

ASU - Hill 2-yard run (Ainsworth kick), eight plays, 33 yards in 3:20

USC - Leinart 1-yard run (Killeen kick), eight plays, 86 yards in 2:41

USC - Jarrett 52-yard pass from Bush (Killeen kick), four plays, 64 yards in 1:57

USC - Jarrett 34-yard pass from Leinart (Killeen kick), one play, 34 yards in 0:07

USC - Killeen 34-yard field goal, 11 plays, 50 yards in 5:23

Team Statistics

	ASU	USC
First Downs	13	23
Rushes-Yards (Net)	30-24	38-145
Passing Yds (Net)	219	301
Passes Att-Comp-Int	39-23-2	28-17-0
Total Offense Plays-Yards	69-243	66-446
Punt Returns-Yards	1-8	2-49
Kickoff Returns-Yards	2-31	1-21
Punts (Number-Avg)	6-41.2	3-48.7
Fumbles-Lost	1-0	1-1
Penalties-Yards	10-50	4-25
Possession Time	30:32	29:28
Sacks by (Number-Yards)	1-10	8-45

Individual Offensive Statistics

Rushing: **Arizona State**-Hill 12-31; Jones 4-18; Burgess 3-13; Keller 3-(-3); Walter, Andrew 8-(-35). **USC**-White 16-68; Kirtman 4-24; Bush 5-21; Dennis 5-19; Webb 4-16; Cassel 1-6; Reed 1-0; Leinart 2-(-9).

Passing: **Arizona State**-Walter 19-34-2-181; Keller 2-3-0-20; MacDonald 1-1-0-26; Burgess 1-1-0-(-8). **USC**-Leinart 13-24-0-224; Cassel 3-3-0-25; Bush 1-1-0-52.

Receiving: **Arizona State**-Miller 8-102; Hagan 5-52; Mutz 2-25; Richardson 2-24; Burgess 2-11; Hill 1-6; Lewis 1-5; Burghgraef 1-2; Walter, Andrew 1-(-8). **USC**-Jarrett 5-139; Byrd 3-49; Bush 2-45; White 2-22; Davis, 2-6; McFoy 1-19; Holmes 1-14; Kirtman 1-7.

Interceptions: **Arizona State**-None. **USC**-Grootegoed 1-41; Bing 1-0.

Sacks (Unassisted-Assisted): **Arizona State**-Davis Jr. 1-0. **USC**-Tatupu 1-0; Nunn 1-0; Team 1-0; Ashton 1-0; Wright 1-0; Rucker 1-0; Jackson 1-0; Cody 1-0.

Tackles (Unassisted-Assisted): **Arizona State**-Robinson 6-5; Stewart 5-1; McKenzie 4-1; Thrower 4-1; Burks 4-1; Williams 2-3; Baker 2-1; Johnson 2-1; Golden 1-2; Green 2-0; Franklin 2-0; Talbot 2-0; Davis Jr. 2-0; Reininger 2-0. **USC**-Sartz 5-2; M. Bing 4-2; Tatupu 2-4; Jackson 4-0; Arbet 3-1; E. Wright 3-0; Thomas 2-1; Wright 1-2; Grootegoed 1-2; Cody 2-0; Rucker 2-0; Team 2-0; Wyatt 2-0.

"I'm surprised we were able to do what we were able to do, but on the other side, I'm thrilled," Carroll said. "We talked about how a lot of people on the outside would look at this as a game we wouldn't be ready for."

From the opening kickoff, USC was ready. The Trojans scored touchdowns on three of their first four possessions, all on passes from quarterback Matt Leinart (13 of 24, 224 yards, four touchdowns).

It was just the kind of easy victory the Trojans usually get under Carroll, except for the previous two games, when USC beat Stanford and Cal by a combined nine points.

"Critics are going to be critics," Leinart said. "Everyone's jumped off the bandwagon because we're not blowing anyone out."

Um, all except the roughly 90,000 apparently.

Whatever stragglers felt doubts probably leapt back on the bandwagon by halftime. Or at least when tailback Reggie Bush took a reverse handoff and calmly threw a 52-yard touchdown pass to Jarrett that gave USC a 35-7 advantage.

"I saw the safety with Dwayne and I was going to run it, but then Dwayne was wide open," Bush said.

Bush caught a touchdown pass, threw one and nearly returned a punt for one. But he stepped out of bounds on a 41-yard return that would have been a touchdown.

"I thought I had it," Bush said. "But the offense was due for a big game. We just felt like we didn't play as good as we should have last week."

You could tell USC played better just by looking at offensive coordinator Norm Chow. Last week, he talked about the "heat" on the offense for being on the field just 50 plays, an all-time low for a Carroll-coached team.

But he was all smiles after routing the Sun Devils (5-1, 2-1).

"What we had was a little sense of urgency," Chow said. "We knew we hadn't played well. I think our team felt it. We challenged our kids to step up."

USC clearly did, while Arizona State clumsily fell down.

"They were walking into the locker room with their heads down and we knew they quit," McFoy said.

Walter, who passed for just 181 yards and threw two interceptions, was at a loss for words.

"I didn't expect this," he said. "I really don't have any answers. They didn't do an awful lot different than they did all year. We just didn't adjust well."

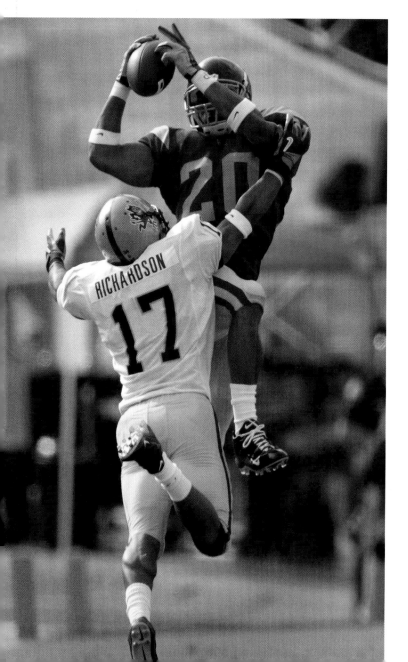

LEFT: Darnell Bing (20) intercepts a pass in the second half. USC's defense sacked ASU eight times and picked off two passes. *Staff photo by Hans Gutknecht*

ABOVE: Dwayne Jarrett (8) and Fred Matua (51) celebrate Jarrett's second-quarter score against ASU.
Staff photo by Hans Gutknecht

Staff photo by Hans Gutknecht

Ho-hum USC Routs Huskies

BY SCOTT WOLF, *STAFF WRITER*

Pete Carroll did everything but make USC write, "I will not let down," 100 times on a blackboard before Saturday's game with Washington, but human nature proved too powerful, even for the No. 1 ranked Trojans.

"I think we just took it lightly. Everyone was relaxed," USC wide receiver Chris McFoy said. "There wasn't a lot of motivation."

You could blame USC for being lackadaisical. You could blame Washington for bringing a 1-5 record into the Coliseum. Or you could blame the schedule for providing USC a bottom-dweller after two top-15 opponents.

Better yet, just blame the offense.

"I think Matt (Leinart) was off, and we were out of sync," offensive coordinator Norm Chow said. "Maybe we came out a little conservative."

But like so much with the Trojans this season, in the end it didn't matter, as they dominated the Huskies 38-0 before 72,855.

It wasn't a victory that won many style points, especially with USC holding a head-scratching 10-0 halftime advantage, with three of those points set up by the defense.

That's not likely to matter much when poll voters and other onlookers check the final score.

It'll look like everything went as planned.

Looks were deceiving Saturday, as USC's offense stumbled and staggered for two quarters while its defense continually stuffed Washington.

"For whatever reason, we were unable to execute the game plan," Leinart said. "Part of that is my fault. I didn't play very well in the first half. I can't dwell on this."

Leinart completed 24-of-43 passes for 217 yards with two touchdowns and an interception, but the stats didn't fully detail the struggles, or the number of times he got hit.

The offensive line did one of its poorer jobs, as Washington blitzed its linebackers effectively and forced Leinart into several bad throws.

"I was a little worried our offense wouldn't kick-start," linebacker Matt Grootegoed said. When a reserved veteran like Grootegoed is concerned, it means a lot of other people are probably asking questions, too.

Fortunately for the Trojans, the offense got its act together at halftime. Fittingly, the defense deserved another huge assist.

On the first play of the second half, Grootegoed hit tailback Kenny James, who fumbled. Defensive end Frostee Rucker recovered at the Washington 18-yard line, and LenDale White scored on a 3-yard run four plays later to put the Trojans ahead 17-0.

Just like that, the nervous edge to the game disappeared, and USC added two more touchdowns in the third quarter to set up a final 12 minutes of garbage time. Another difference in

LEFT: Reggie Bush (5) ran for 55 yards and caught six passes in the shutout victory. *Staff photo by Hans Gutknecht*

	1	2	3	4	Score
Washington	0	0	0	0	0
USC	0	10	21	7	38

Scoring Summary
USC - Killeen 29-yard field goal, 4 plays, -5 yards in 2:11
USC - Bush 15-yard pass from Leinart (Killeen kick), 8 plays, 83 yards in 3:12
USC - White 3-yard run (Killeen kick), 4 plays, 18 yards in 1:17
USC - Mitchell 29-yard pass from Leinart (Killeen kick), four plays, 52 yards in 1:17
USC - White 2-yard run (Killeen kick), 12 plays, 62 yards in 4:26
USC - Reed 28-yard run (Killeen kick), eight plays, 86 yards in 3:47

Team Statistics
	WASH	USC
First Downs	6	28
Rushes-Yards (Net)	27-50	42-197
Passing Yards (Net)	63	256
Passes Att-Comp-Int	28-7-1	48-28-1
Total Offense Plays-Yards	55-113	90-453
Punt Returns-Yards	0-0	2-31
Kickoff Returns-Yards	1-12	0-0
Punts (Number-Avg)	10-42.9	3-48.3
Fumbles-Lost	2-2	1-1
Penalties-Yards	9-60	5-30
Possession Time	20:51	39:09
Sacks by (Number-Yards)	3-12	1-6

Individual Offensive Statistics
Rushing: **Washington**-Sampson 11-37; James 7-18; Stanback 9-(-5). **USC**-White 17-93; Bush 13-55; Reed 1-28; Dennis 4-12; Cassel 2-12; Griffin 2-9; Leinart 3-(-12).

Passing: **Washington**-Stanback 3-16-0-27; Paus 4-12-1-36. **USC**-Leinart 24-43-1-217; Cassel 4-5-0-39.

Receiving: **Washington**-Whithorne 2-22; Toledo 2-16; Russo 1-10; Lewis 1-8; Lyon 1-7. **USC**-Bush 6-41; Byrd 5-57; Jarrett 5-31; McFoy 2-26; White 2-18; Mitchell 1-29; Walker 1-22; Adewale 1-16; Kirtman 1-9; Davis 1-9; Reed 1-2; Buchanon 1-(-1); Holmes 1-(-3).

Individual Defensive Statistics
Interceptions: **Washington**-Wallace 1-7. **USC**-Rivers 1-22.

Sacks (Unassisted-Assisted): **Washington**-Hopoi 3-0. **USC**-Jackson 1-0.

Tackles (Unassisted-Assisted): **Washington**-Wallace 6-2; Lobendahn 4-4; White 6-1; Hopoi 6-0; Goldson 5-1; Benjamin 3-2; Galloway 4-0; Johnson 4-0; Fountaine 3-0; Mapuolesega 3-0; Ala 3-0; Newell 2-1; Hemphill 2-1; Afoa 2-0. **USC**-Grootegoed 3-2; Rivers 2-2; Cody 2-2; Tatupu 1-3; Rucker 2-1; Leach 1-2; Schweiger 0-3; Wyatt 2-0; Williams 2-0.

the improved second half was that USC jettisoned some plays to capitalize on Washington's loose defense.

"They were playing 20 yards off me," McFoy said. "We made some corrections."

As exasperating as USC's offense played, the defense was another matter. It seemed like

Washington wouldn't score had it played another four quarters.

"I thought after the first quarter, we were in great shape for this game," Carroll said. "This is the best defense we've played since we've been here. The last three to four weeks we were so much different than in the season opener against Virginia Tech."

USC's defensive performance probably meant more in Seattle, because the Huskies' streak of games without being shut out, the nation's longest, ended at 271. Washington was last held without a point in 1981.

"It's part of our history," Washington quarterback Isaiah Stanback said. "It's part of the reason people come here to play. You don't want to be part of the team that ends that streak."

Stanback, making his first college start, completed just three of 16 passes for 27 yards. Things were going so poorly that when Washington inserted quarterback Casey Paus, the public address announcer called him Cory Paus, referring to Casey's older brother, who played for UCLA.

Washington (1-6, 0-4) is guaranteed its first losing season since 1976, former coach Don James' second season.

"They look the part, and that's what a No. 1 team looks like," Huskies coach Keith Gilbertson said of the Trojans.

With the USC offense offering a ho-hum performance, the defense provided highlights. Besides Grootegoed's forced fumble, freshman linebacker Keith Rivers intercepted his first career pass, and Rucker also forced a fumble.

"Something is kind of building," Grootegoed said. "A lot of players are making plays and playing bigger than they usually do."

It'll surely mean a lot to Carroll, who doubles as defensive coordinator and can put the heat on the offense this week, much like he did following its inconsistent effort against California.

"We were forced to deal with a lot of first-half offensive frustration," Carroll said. "It feels good to get a shutout. There is a pride factor involved. It's nice to see the players fight for it."

BELOW: Lawrence Jackson (96) teams with Shaun Cody to record a sack. *Staff photo by Evan Yee*

ABOVE: USC mobs Washington QB Isaiah Stanback for a first-quarter sack, one of eight for the defense.
Staff photo by Hans Gutknecht

Northwest Conquest

BY SCOTT WOLF, *STAFF WRITER*

PULLMAN, Wash.—Sometimes, in the postgame euphoria of the locker room, the truth escapes from the programmed responses that football usually produces.

"We're going to play Auburn now, if they win out," USC tailback Reggie Bush said, minutes after the No. 1 Trojans routed Washington State 42-12 in front of 35,117 at Martin Stadium.

A rare and refreshing forward-looking comment regarding national championship possibilities, after USC coach Pete Carroll told Bush that North Carolina upset No. 3 Miami.

Does this mean Carroll, who religiously ignores the Bowl Championship Series rankings, actually score-watches?

"I didn't even know, someone just told me that score, is it true?" he said with his usual charm.

The brief outburst of candor was justified, however, because it's getting harder and harder to figure out who can challenge USC.

The elements gave their best shot Saturday afternoon but were dispatched quicker than Washington State.

A hailstorm hit during warm-ups, and Cougars fans screamed their approval, hopeful the weather might even up the odds.

"I've never seen snow before," USC offensive tackle Sam Baker said.

Instead of shrinking, the Trojans embraced the freakish storm.

"I thought I was in New England," wide receiver Chris McFoy added. "Now I can say I played in semi-slush."

Carroll was thrilled his players reacted giddily to the hail and worried it might incite the fans.

"The crowd was trying to stick it to us there and we took the opposite approach," he said. "I think the Washington State fans thought that was going to do something to our guys. Instead, it was all these Orange County boys letting them know they could get out there and let them know it was going to be a fun night."

Unfortunately, the pregame storm departed before kickoff, perhaps bored at the prospect of what was about to ensue.

Washington State (3-5, 1-4 Pacific-10 Conference) opened the game with a disastrous onside kick that traveled two yards. That gave the Trojans the ball on the Cougars' 37-yard line and four plays later, Bush sprinted 19 yards around the right side for a touchdown.

USC kicker Ryan Killeen then pooched the kickoff, which an unprepared Washington State return unit failed to field, and Desmond Reed recovered at the 21-yard line. Two penalties later, the Trojans were at Washington State's 4, and LenDale White eventually scored on a 1-yard run.

"We hadn't started playing, and it was 14-0," Carroll said.

About this time, it appeared some fans were already heading home.

Opposite: Matt Leinart showed deadly accuracy against Washington State, completing 23 of 28 passes. *Otto Greule Jr./Getty Images*

	1	2	3	4	Score
USC	21	14	7	0	42
Washington State	0	0	12	0	12

Scoring Summary

USC - Bush 19-yard run (Killeen kick), five plays, 37 yards in 1:51
USC - White 1-yard run (Killeen kick), two plays, 21 yards in 0:46
USC - Bush 57-yard punt return (Killeen kick)
USC - Jarrett 42-yard pass from Leinart (Killeen kick), 10 plays, 94 yards in 3:48
USC - White 7-yard run (Killeen kick), five plays, 18 yards in 2:35
USC - Jarrett 4-yard pass from Leinart (Killeen kick), 12 plays, 55 yards in 5:25
WSU - Bumpus 24-yard pass from Brink (Langley kick failed), three plays, 24 yards in 0:44
WSU - Bennett 28-yard interception return (Brink pass intercepted)

Team Statistics

	USC	WSU
First Downs	26	11
Rushes-Yards (Net)	54-186	25-(-9)
Passing Yards (Net)	235	165
Passes Att-Comp-Int	30-23-1	40-17-1
Total Offense Plays-Yards	84-421	65-156
Punt Returns-Yards	4-94	3-19
Kickoff Returns-Yards	1-7	2-27
Punts (Number-Avg)	6-37.3	9-41.2
Fumbles-Lost	3-2	7-3
Penalties-Yards	8-75	8-72
Possession Time	38:54	21:06
Sacks By (Number-Yards)	5-30	2-14

Individual Offensive Statistics

Rushing: **USC**-White 16-77; Dennis 11-55; Bush 14-42; Reed 9-27; Cassel 3-(-7); Leinart 1-(-8). **Washington State**-Basler 1-17; Harrison 11-15; Thompson 3-0; Jordan, Chris 1-(-4); Team 1-(-18); Brink 8-(-19).

Passing: **USC**-Leinart 23-28-0-235; Cassel 0-2-1-0. **Washington State**-Brink 17-40-1-165.

Receiving: **USC**-Byrd 5-32; Bush 5-23; Jarrett 4-64; McFoy 3-54; Holmes 2-20; Kirtman 2-12; Mitchell 1-33; Reed 1-(-3). **Washington State**-Bumpus 6-68; Hill 5-62; Jordan 2-23; Martin 1-5; Harvey 1-3; Taylor 1-3; Harrison 1-1.

Individual Defensive Statistics

Interceptions: **USC**-Thomas 1-0. **Washington State**-Bennett 1-28.

Sacks (Unassisted-Assisted): **USC**-Patterson 0-1; Grootegoed 1-0; Cody 1-0; Sartz 0-1; Tatupu 1-0; Williams 1-0. **Washington State**-Derting 1-1; Bruce 0-1.

Tackles (Unassisted-Assisted): **USC** -Grootegoed 4-2; Sartz 3-2; Bing 3-2; Tatupu 3-2; Wyatt 3-0; Arbet 2-1; Nunn 1-2; Farr 2-0; Leach 2-0. **Washington State**-Derting 8-6; Bohannon 11-2; Bruce 3-6; Abdullah 3-5; Davis 4-2; Braidwood 3-3; Cook 3-3; Frampton 3-2; Bennett 2-3; Paymah 3-1; Pitoitua 2-1; Dildine 2-1.

"You could look at the sideline, and one of their players tried to get the crowd into it and nobody responded," White said.

From there, the Trojans (8-0, 5-0) kept rolling as Matt Leinart (23 of 28, 235 yards, two touchdowns) calmly dissected the defense with

ABOVE: Chris McFoy (82) hauled in three passes and 54 yards in the USC blowout victory.
Otto Greule Jr./Getty Images

short passes in the first half, completing five passes to Bush and four to tight end Dominique Byrd.

Bush returned a punt 57 yards for a touchdown, undoubtedly reviving his Heisman Trophy hopes, and Leinart connected with Dwayne Jarrett on a 42-yard touchdown pass that gave the Trojans a 28-0 lead early in the second quarter.

The only remaining question concerned USC's chances of posting a third consecutive shutout. But that disappeared abruptly when Carroll emptied the bench, and reserve quarterback Matt Cassel had a nightmarish cameo in the third quarter. He fumbled the snap on his first play, and Washington State recovered at USC's 24-yard line.

The Cougars scored on a 24-yard pass from Alex Brink to Michael Bumpus as Carroll chewed out Cassel on the sideline. Cassel's next play was a rollout, and his pass was tipped by fullback David Kirtman and intercepted by linebacker Pat Bennett, who returned it 28 yards for a touchdown.

Cassel fumbled a snap on the next series, and Carroll had seen enough. In a move that raised some eyebrows, he returned Leinart to protect a 42-12 fourth-quarter lead.

"That one little spurt was a mess," Carroll said. "I wanted the game to go smoothly, and we were struggling."

Carroll said he would have used third-string quarterback Brandon Hance, but Hance got hit in the forehead by a punted ball Friday night and required stitches.

"I have no idea how it happened, but it hurt," Hance said.

Leinart wasn't the only starter sent back in, and not everyone was quite sure what to make of it, especially some of the starters.

"I really didn't know what was going on," Byrd said. "We were having a little trouble with snaps. That's something you have to do sometimes."

White, who gained 77 yards in 16 carries, said, "I really wouldn't recommend (putting the starters back in), but you have to do what you have to do."

Above: Desmond Reed (22) and Josh Pinkard (36) celebrate after recovering a Washington State fumble.
Otto Greule Jr./Getty Images

#11 MATT LEINART

BY SCOTT WOLF, *STAFF WRITER*

Matt Leinart replaced Carson Palmer as USC's quarterback, but he almost did it two years earlier than anyone realized.

Although Palmer is considered perhaps the greatest quarterback in school history, he struggled during the 2001 season and Leinart almost replaced him late in the year against Arizona.

"He was going to play the whole second half against Arizona," said Leinart's father, Bob. "Then while we were driving to Arizona, Matt called and said they decided they didn't want to burn his redshirt year. They chose not to play him.

"Because if Carson went 14 for 14 the next game, Matt would have burned his redshirt year with one half."

That Arizona game turned out to be the start of a five-game winning streak for the Trojans and delayed Leinart taking over for Palmer by two years.

"It seems like yesterday. My whole career feels like a month," Leinart said. I feel like Carson was here last month. All those days when you're playing and winning, everything goes by fast."

It's hard to believe Leinart won the Heisman if you go back before the 2002 season, when he was unhappy about the number of snaps he got in practice as the Trojans' No. 3 quarterback.

"That was a long time and a lot of stress ago," Bob Leinart said. "It happened for a reason. He wasn't in the right mental state. He was mentally prepared. He wanted to get a shot. That was the hardest part for him at USC. He just wanted a shot. But they made the decision if Carson got hurt and needed a quick fix, (Matt) Cassel would be the guy."

Leinert's father met with USC offensive coordinator Norm Chow on several occasions over the few snaps his son received, and Leinart didn't rule out the possibility of transferring. But all of that changed once Palmer departed.

"He made a huge improvement in spring practice this year," Chow said. "Everything changed. He grew and became a leader. He's flourished since becoming a starter."

Leinart became the Trojans' sixth Heisman Trophy winner, cruising to an easier-than-expected victory over Oklahoma tailback Adrian Peterson and quarterback Jason White.

Leinart is USC's second Heisman winner in three seasons, following Palmer's 2002 victory.

"I remember watching Carson win it while sitting on my couch," Leinart said. "I could never imagine. I'm living a dream. I'm still living a dream."

Although a tight race was expected, Leinart won comfortably with 1,325 points, while Peterson finished second with 997. White was third (957); Utah quarterback Alex Smith fourth (635) and USC tailback Reggie Bush fifth (597). Leinart won five of the six voting regions, losing only the Southwest, where Oklahoma is located. It's the first time in Heisman voting that two sets of teammates finished in the top five.

Leinart finished with 66 percent of the top-five votes while Peterson received 58 and White 53. USC also tied Ohio State for second place with six Heisman winners. Notre Dame leads all schools with seven.

Instead of wondering if he'll transfer, people now worry Leinart might turn pro after the season. Much like when discussing the Heisman, Leinart tries to take the high road.

"It's going to be interesting to see," Leinart said about his pro stock. "I stick to my word. I plan on coming back. I'm firm in my decision now."

But in the next breath, Leinart admits his mind is open to change.

"Fifteen million reasons would be tough to turn down," Leinart said. "If you've got that, you go. Anyone in my position would be curious. But I think that's highly unlikely.

Class: *Redshirt Junior*
Hometown: *Santa Ana, California*
High School: *Mater Dei*
Major: *Sociology*
Position: *Quarterback*
Height: *6'5"*
Weight: *225*

Coast Is Barely Clear

BY SCOTT WOLF, *STAFF WRITER*

CORVALLIS, Ore.—A dense fog enveloped Reser Stadium on Saturday night, but it was nothing compared to the haze top-ranked USC appeared to be in from the outset against Oregon State.

The Beavers scored the first 13 points and seemed in danger of pulling off a major upset.

Although the fog looked horrible on TV, it wasn't quite that bad on the field, although you wouldn't know from the way the Trojans started. USC fumbled twice and quarterback Matt Leinart threw an interception as the Trojans joined No. 2 Oklahoma and No. 4 California in nail-biters.

But the fog didn't last forever, and neither did USC's funk. The Trojans scored four consecutive touchdowns to wear down the Beavers 28-20 in front of 36,412.

"I was hoping we wouldn't be in a game like this because everybody else was," USC coach Pete Carroll said, referring to the close games for other top teams.

The turning point was a 65-yard punt return by Reggie Bush that gave USC a 21-13 lead with 12:27 left in the game and eased

thoughts the Trojans (9-0, 6-0) might lose for the first time in the shrouded conditions.

"It was really a magical night," Carroll said. "It's like we played in a cloud. I'm glad the cloud had a silver lining."

It didn't have to be that difficult, but USC's offense certainly seemed out of sync in the first half.

A couple examples: Somehow, the Trojans got a delay-of-game penalty after linebacker Lofa Tatupu intercepted a pass in the third quarter. And in the second quarter, wide receiver John Walker got yanked off the field right before the snap on one play to avoid having 12 players on the field.

To add to the woes, kicker Ryan Killeen missed a 45-yard field goal and had another attempt blocked.

"I wasn't nervous," Tatupu said. "Stanford had us worse."

But even with those problems, Leinart's two touchdown passes to tight end Dominique Byrd provided a razor-thin 14-13 lead in the fourth quarter before Bush's heroics.

Byrd, chastised by Carroll on Friday for making too many one-handed catches in practice, caught a 25-yard touchdown pass with two hands to give the Trojans a one-point lead with 12:14 remaining in the third quarter. It was USC's first lead of the game.

"I tried to catch every ball with two hands because of what he said, but it wasn't possible every play," Byrd said.

Previously, Byrd got a measure of satisfaction by making a terrific one-handed catch on an 18-yard touchdown pass in the second quarter that cut Oregon State's lead to 13-7.

The Beavers (4-5, 3-3) were ready from the outset and sometimes a little lucky as a strange play contributed to their first touchdown. Quarterback Derek Anderson completed a 37-

yard pass to tight end Joe Newton, who was stripped of the ball by safety Darnell Bing. But wide receiver Mike Hass recovered and ran an additional 14 yards.

LEFT: Tight end Dominque Byrd reaches for extra yards. He was the Trojans' leading receiver with seven catches and 85 yards. *Otto Greule Jr./Getty Images*

	1	2	3	4	Score
USC	0	7	7	14	28
Oregon State	6	7	0	7	20

Scoring Summary

OSU - Serna 25-yard field goal, six plays, 11 yards in 2:34
OSU - Serna 33-yard field goal, five plays, 40 yards in 0:45
OSU - Love 8-yard pass from Anderson (Serna kick), seven plays, 65 yards in 1:48
USC - Byrd 18-yard pass from Leinart (Killeen kick), five plays, 77 yards in 1:34
USC - Byrd 25-yard pass from Leinart (Killeen kick), seven plays, 50 yards in 1:40
USC - Bush 65-yard punt return (Killeen kick)
USC - White 5-yard run (Killeen kick), seven plays, 77 yards in 3:50
OSU - Hawkins 36-yard pass from Anderson (Serna kick), nine plays, 84 yards in 0:55

Team Statistics

	USC	OSU
First Downs	20	22
Rushes-Yards (Net)	44-210	25-34
Passing Yards (Net)	205	330
Passes Att-Comp-Int	31-17-1	51-22-2
Total Offense Plays-Yards	75-415	76-364
Punt Returns-Yards	3-73	3-19
Kickoff Returns-Yards	4-114	5-93
Punts (Number-Avg)	7-43.1	8-46.5
Fumbles-Lost	4-2	2-1
Penalties-Yards	6-50	4-35
Possession Time	32:39	27:21
Sacks By (Number-Yards)	4-29	2-6

Individual Offensive Statistics

Rushing: **USC**-White 25-116; Bush 11-88; Leinart 5-12; Team 3-(-6).
Oregon State-Wright 12-60; Cole 4-(-3); Anderson 9-(-23).

Passing: **USC**-Leinart 17-31-1-205.
Oregon State-Anderson 22-51-2-330.

Receiving: **USC**-Byrd 7-85; Holmes 3-60; Jarrett 2-21; Bush 2-6; Kirtman 1-17; Mitchell 1-11; White 1-5.
Oregon State-Hass 8-119; Love 5-71; Newton 4-75; Wheat-Brown 3-31; Hawkins 1-36; Wright 1-(-2).

Individual Defensive Statistics

Interceptions: **USC**-Tatupu 1-2; Leach 1-14.
Oregon State-Meeuwsen 1-0.

Sacks (Unassisted-Assisted): **USC**-Cody 1-0; Patterson 0-1; Tatupu 1-0; Grootegoed 1-0; Wyatt 0-1.
Oregon State-Swancutt 2-0.

Tackles (Unassisted-Assisted): **USC**-Grootegoed 6-3; Wyatt 6-2; Patterson 2-5; Cody 4-1; Bing 4-1; Sartz 2-3; Jackson 1-4; Tatupu 4-0; Leach 4-0; Lua 2-0.
Oregon State-Bray 5-7; Meeuwsen 7-4; Swancutt 5-5; Piscitelli 6-1; Williams 1-4; Scott 3-1; Smith 1-3; Anderson 1-3; Van Orsow 0-4; Ellison 0-4; Browner 3-0; Davidson 2-0.

That set up Anderson's 8-yard touchdown pass to Marcel Love over the middle and gave the Beavers a 13-0 advantage.

Typical of close games, the Trojans' special teams faltered. Killeen's 43-yard field-goal attempt was easily blocked by Mitch Meeuswen, who strolled right through a hole in the line.

That wasn't the only miscue. For the third time in four games, Bush fumbled a punt and it led to the Beavers' first score. Bush signaled for a fair catch, but the ball went right through his hands and was recovered by Oregon State's Gerard Lawson at the Trojans' 18-yard line.

The Beavers reached the 3 before the drive stalled and settled for a 25-yard field goal by Alexis Serna and a 3-0 lead.

Oregon State added another field goal after Anderson completed a 25-yard pass to Hass and a 15-yard penalty on defensive end Frostee Rucker for roughing the passer. Serna converted a 33-yard attempt to give the Beavers a 6-0 lead with 1:41 left in the quarter.

The Trojans barely had the ball in the first quarter, running just nine plays as the Beavers dominated time of possession, 10:02 to 4:58.

Bush also fumbled in the second quarter after catching a pass, but officials ruled he was down. Replays indicated he lost control of the ball before hitting the ground.

The sophomore electrified the crowd on the next possession, though, by taking a reverse handoff and eluding three tackles for a 44-yard gain.

That play provided USC with its first touchdown. Leinart threw 18 yards over the middle to Byrd, who made a one-handed catch as he dove in the end zone. It was the first sign of life in USC's offense and cut Oregon State's lead to 13-7.

As the half concluded, USC drove toward a potential game-leading touchdown, but Leinart's pass intended for Jason Mitchell was intercepted by Meeuswen.

Leinart completed 17 of 31 passes for 205 yards with two touchdowns and one interception. Anderson was 22 of 51 for 330 yards, two touchdowns and one interception.

LEFT: It was a close game played in a heavy fog, but Matt Leinart and the Trojans were able to celebrate their ninth victory of the season. *AP/WWP*

ABOVE: Dominque Byrd stretches to catch his first of two touchdowns. *AP/WWP*

Sloppy USC Romps Again

BY SCOTT WOLF, *STAFF WRITER*

The idea of top-ranked USC playing lowly Arizona didn't sound terribly appealing, even to Trojans tight end Fred Davis.

The freshman was suspended from the game for negative academic performance and decided to go home to Ohio for the weekend. Whether or not he returns will be determined this week. But he didn't miss much, other than the fact the Trojans officially clinched a Rose Bowl bid with the victory.

USC played one of its sloppiest games of the season, then regrouped late in third quarter and routed Arizona 49-9 in front of 80,167 on Saturday night at the Coliseum.

The Trojans held an oh-so-embarrassing 21-9 lead after Arizona quarterback Richard Kovalcheck threw a nine-yard touchdown pass to tight end Steve Fleming with 4:55 left in the third quarter.

And one of the main reasons for that close score was turnovers. Although Coach Pete Carroll promised to hassle the Trojans about protecting the ball, USC fumbled three times as quarterback Matt Leinart, tailback Reggie Bush and fullback Lee Webb all lost the ball.

Staff photo by Andy Holzman

ABOVE: Matt Leinhart scrambles to complete one of his 27 passes. *Staff photo by Andy Holzman*

Bush fumbled in his fifth consecutive game.

"This makes me sick," Carroll said. "We threw the ball on the ground. We've got to take care of it."

It didn't cost the Trojans on Saturday, but it could have if they played a better opponent. Much like the kicking game, it remains some-thing that could become a major issue if USC (10-0, 7-0) gets into a close game against Notre Dame and UCLA, or perhaps in a bowl game.

Speaking of bowl games, each USC player received a rose after the game, symbolizing the Rose Bowl, although every player would rather be holding an orange in two games.

"You've got to crawl before you can walk," defensive end Lawrence Jackson said.

Bush added: "It's our first goal, but we have two more games left and now we're playing for the national championship. We haven't talked about the national championship, but we know it's there."

Tailback LenDale White (119 yards), who often acts as the Trojans' safety net, bailed out USC after Arizona's third-quarter touchdown, by springing a 54-yard run that helped set up his own touchdown on a 6-yard run. That gave USC a 28-6 advantage.

Leinart then put the game away with a 44-yard pass to receiver Dwayne Jarrett, followed immediately by a 13-yard touchdown pass to Jarrett for a 35-6 USC advantage.

Things degenerated further when linebacker Dallas Sartz tipped a Kovalcheck pass, which was intercepted by cornerback Justin Wyatt and returned to the Arizona 20-yard line.

Leinart hooked up with Jarrett again, on a 12-yard pass, to give the Trojans a 42-9 advantage that unsuspecting poll voters will think was another routine blowout.

Before that 21-0 spurt, however, the Trojans weren't generating many style points for toying with the Wildcats (2-8, 1-6).

"I don't know where to start," Arizona coach Mike Stoops said. "USC is a very good football team. We got outmanned, outplayed and outcoached. That's why they're the No. 1 team in the country."

In an indication of the offense's early frustration, the best pass of the first half came from reserve tailback Desmond Reed, who lined up at receiver and took the ball on a reverse before throwing a 55-yard pass to Jarrett. On the next play, White scored on a 3-yard run to give USC a 14-3 lead with 2:54 left in the half.

One play typified the first half when Leinart fumbled on fourth-and-one at the 30-yard line with 27 seconds left in the half and Arizona safety Dominic Patrick recovered. That kept the first half relatively close, and the mar-gin was almost identical to USC's 10-point half-time lead over Washington three weeks ago.

Leinart finished completing 27 of 35 passes for 280 yards and three touchdowns.

	1	2	3	4	Score
Arizona	3	0	6	0	9
USC	0	14	21	14	49

Scoring Summary

ARIZ - Folk 48-yard field goal, six plays, 41 yards in 1:54
USC - Kirtman 5-yard pass from Leinart (Killeen kick), 12 plays, 57 yards in 6:07
USC - White 3-yard run (Killeen kick), five plays, 71 yards in 2:18
USC - White 2-yard run (Killeen kick), 11 plays, 76 yards in 5:15
ARIZ - Fleming 9-yard pass from Kovalcheck (Kovalcheck pass failed), two plays, 40 yards in 0:18
USC - White 6-yard run (Killeen kick), five plays, 78 yards in 1:35
USC - Jarrett 13-yard pass from Leinart (Killeen kick), two plays, 57 yards in 0:31
USC - Jarrett 12-yard pass from Leinart (Killeen kick), five plays, 20 yards in 2:40
USC - Dennis 1-yard run (Killeen kick), eight plays, 65 yards in 3:43

Team Statistics

	ARIZ	USC
First Downs	14	25
Rushes-Yards (Net)	25-90	38-216
Passing Yards (Net)	165	369
Passes Att-Comp-Int	32-15-2	40-31-0
Total Offense Plays-Yards	57-255	78-585
Punt Returns-Yards	2-4	1-1
Kickoff Returns-Yards	4-78	3-65
Punts (Number-Avg)	8-38.4	2-44.5
Fumbles-Lost	0-0	4-3
Penalties-Yards	3-20	6-46
Possession Time	26:12	33:48
Sacks By (Number-Yards)	1-7	3-27

Individual Offensive Statistics

Rushing: **Arizona**-Bell 15-74; Steptoe 1-31; Henry 3-3; Team 1-(-2); Kovalcheck 5-(-16).
USC-White 16-118; Bush 12-45; Reed 2-37; Leinart 3-7; Dennis 3-5; Woodert 1-4; Hance 1-0.

Passing: **Arizona**-Kovalcheck 15-32-2-165.
USC-Leinart 27-35-0-280; Cassel 2-3-0-28; Reed 1-1-0-55; Hance 1-1-0-6.

Receiving: **Arizona**-Bell 4-9; Fleming 3-35; Steptoe 3-27; Jefferson 1-25; McRae 1-24; Ealy 1-23; Williams 1-13; Limon 1-9.
USC-Byrd 8-72; Jarrett 6-144; Mitchell 5-74; Bush 4-19; Holmes 3-21; Buchanon 2-11; Webb 1-22; Kirtman 1-5; Reed 1-1.

Individual Defensive Statistics

Interceptions: **Arizona**-None.
USC-Wyatt 1-19; Jackson 1-19.

Sacks (Unassisted-Assisted): **Arizona**-Means 1-0.
USC-Grootegoed 0-2; Tatupu 1-1; Bing 0-1.

Tackles (Unassisted-Assisted): **Arizona**-Johnson 9-0; Howard 7-1; Fontenot 6-2; Cason 5-2; Krogstad 4-3; Means 4-1; Smith 4-0; Torrey 3-1; Wingate 3-0; Williams 3-0.
USC-Tatupu 5-6; Bing 4-2; Grootegoed 2-4; Wright 3-1; Leach 1-3; Ting 2-1; Rivers 2-1; Ashton 1-2; Gomez 2-0; Wyatt 2-0.

ABOVE: Reggie Bush tries to fight through an Arizona tackle. *Staff photo by Andy Holzman*

As unlikely as it seemed before the game, the Trojans actually trailed the Wildcats 3-0 in the first quarter, as Nick Folk kicked a 48-yard field goal. Kovalcheck, making just his fourth career start, played with poise, completing six of 10 passes for 77 yards in the first quarter.

The Trojans eventually struck back, as Leinart threw a 5-yard pass to fullback David Kirtman for a 7-3 advantage. But much like the home game against Washington three weeks ago, USC didn't look terribly excited about the match-up.

Kicker Ryan Killeen continued his slump, badly missing a 27-yard field-goal attempt in the first quarter, his fourth miss in the past five attempts. He has made just seven of 16 field goals this season.

Again, tight end Dominique Byrd remained a prolific part of the Trojans' offense. Byrd caught six passes for 48 yards in the half and was USC's leading receiver.

ABOVE: Dwayne Jarrett fights for additional yardage during a 55-yard option play. *Staff photo by Andy Holzman*

#99 MIKE PATTERSON

BY RICH HAMMOND, *STAFF WRITER*

Mike Patterson wasn't a can't-miss, blue-chip prospect when USC signed him out of high school. There was considerable debate within the coaching staff about whether to award him a scholarship, doubts that turned to fears when Patterson showed up massively overweight to a summer all-star game.

"When we signed him, he was 265 (pounds) and explosive, but then he got up to 325," USC assistant coach Ed Orgeron said. "He played in that all-star game and he didn't look very good. It was a hot day, and he really struggled. Coach Carroll called me up and said, 'Who is this guy you signed? What's going on?' But he trusted my decision. He said, 'Can he play?' and I said, 'Yeah, we'll get him there.'

"After about two or three weeks with us, he started getting in shape, and you could see his hands and feet and the quickness we saw in camp, and you knew he was going to be a good one."

What the Trojans have now, three years later, is a potential All-America senior nose tackle who was named the national Defensive Player of the Week for his 10-tackle effort against Cal. Opponents who before might have dismissed him because of his size now are forced to pay attention.

"It's one of those things where you look back and go, 'Jeez,'" Patterson said. "I never expected to be where I'm at right now. Now if I keep working hard, hopefully things will get even better."

It's hard to imagine exactly how, since Patterson already is close to the complete package. The quick hands and feet that Orgeron noticed immediately were bolstered by the years Patterson spent as a wrestler at Los Alamitos High and now serve as the basis for his success.

Patterson, now at 290 pounds, has a height disadvantage against every opposing lineman, but it's not a problem because he has the speed and strength to get around them.

"You've got to have both," Patterson said. "Wherever your hands go, that's where your feet will go, but you have to have your feet in order to keep moving when your hands are working. It's all technique, and you have to be able to work both of them."

The full range of Patterson's skills was most evident on the first play of the fourth quarter against Cal, with USC clinging to a six-point lead. As Cal quarterback Aaron Rodgers dropped back, Patterson bullrushed around lineman Aaron Merz without breaking stride and sacked Rodgers.

Before the two players hit the ground, Patterson had pulled the ball out of Rodgers' hands, giving USC the ball at the Cal 34. USC's offense didn't score, but neither did Cal for the rest of the game.

"Mike had a terrific game against Cal," Carroll said. "He was active and made big plays on third and fourth downs. He is always a factor. He has great quickness and a great motor, so when the opportunity presents itself, he makes the plays.

"He has a great work ethic and is always bringing it every day. He is the most consistent guy in the time that we have been here. He is a terrific performer and prospect for the next level."

Patterson has undergone a steady progression since Orgeron worked him into shape in that first training camp. As a backup, Patterson played in all but one game in his freshman season, then was tabbed as a starting defensive tackle for the 2002 opener against Auburn, a game in which he recorded eight tackles.

Since then, Patterson has been a stalwart. He hasn't missed a single game because of injury, and playing alongside guys such as Cody, Omar Nazel and Kenechi Udeze brought out his personality.

Patterson isn't effusive by any means—he offers an embarrassed chuckle when asked to talk about his own game—but he has become a team leader who isn't afraid to speak up in the locker room.

"Coaches here are always telling me to speak up, to talk it up and that sort of thing. I understand where they're

Class: *Senior*
Hometown: *Los Alamitos, California*
High School: *Los Alamitos*
Major: *Sociology*
Position: *Defensive Tackle*
Height: *6'0"*
Weight: *290*

coming from. The young guys look up to us older guys and we do have to talk it up."

Now there's plenty to say about Patterson, who goes by the moniker of "Baby Sapp" because his favorite player is Oakland Raiders defensive tackle Warren Sapp. Patterson might not share many personality traits with the bombastic Sapp, but the on-field similarities are becoming increasingly obvious.

"It's definitely awesome to see Mike getting the attention he deserves," said Cody, a four-year teammate. "He's been such a force around college football for the last two years, and a lot of people don't give him credit because he's six feet tall. That's ridiculous because he plays great football."

Staff photo by Andy Holzman

Glorious Day Lives On

BY STEVE DILBECK, *STAFF WRITER*

It was just one afternoon, another college football game played out on a Saturday at the Coliseum 30 long years ago. Only it changed a life forever, if not lives.

Anthony Davis has never needed a reminder, but they're always there. Always waiting, always with another surprise. "Seems everyone I talk to was there," Davis said. "I met one woman who said, 'I was pregnant and when you brought that kickoff back, and you induced my labor.'"

Then there is the woman who emerged from the darkness outside the top of the tunnel following the game, brandishing a crucifix and placing it directly in his face.

"Nobody does that to Notre Dame," she said. "You have to be the devil."

And there are the people who will see him, smile, point and simply say:

"Notre Dame."

If ever one player was identified with a single game, it is Anthony Davis and the USC-Notre Dame game of 1974. Davis set all kinds of NCAA records as a Trojan, should have won the Heisman, enjoyed a long professional career.

Yet it is always about Notre Dame that afternoon, when USC fell behind 24-0 to the Irish only to stage the most remarkable comeback in college football history.

When Davis scored four consecutive touchdowns. When USC scored 55 unanswered points against the No. 1 defense in the nation. When eyes were left so disbelieving, that even to this day, it seems hard to imagine it was seen.

The Trojans rode the stunning 55-24 victory into the Rose Bowl, beat Ohio State and captured the national championship.

It all turned on that stunning afternoon, and Davis doesn't need a calendar to know what time of year it is. His phone always starts ringing before the Notre Dame game, even more this year on its 30th anniversary.

Davis, the former San Fernando High School star, is 52 now. He lives in Irvine, has owned a construction company for years and has lived almost an entire life since that Saturday afternoon.

And still . . .

"I don't know an athlete in America that gets interviewed every year like me," he said. "It's been like this for me for 30 years. Every month in November or December, for a full week the press talks to me.

"I don't care where I am in the country, they find me. Once in 1985, I was up in Stallion Springs, 50 miles outside of Bakersfield, and they found me at the construction site. I couldn't believe it."

Staff photo by David Sprague

But disbelief has always been a part of it. A comeback that seemed part magic, now part legend.

Unbeaten Notre Dame had simply dominated the afternoon. Rolled out to a 24-0 lead with 53 seconds left in the half.

Then quarterback Pat Haden led a lightning drive, hitting Shelton Diggs with a couple of passes before Davis scored on a 7-yard swing pass.

Still, it was 24-6 at the half, and the Irish seemed firmly in control. Davis had cut his left palm in the second quarter and missed most of the coaches' talks at the half while in the training room. He heard head coach John McKay address the entire team at the end.

"All of a sudden, he said, 'They're going to kick the ball to A.D., and he's going to bring it all the way back,'" Davis said. "Just like that. I looked at him like he was a crazy man."

The Trojans were already on the field when Davis left the training room and entered the tunnel just behind the entire Notre Dame team.

"One of them turns and yells, 'We're going to kick the ball to Davis, and we're going to kick his (butt),'" Davis said. "I come from the streets of Pacoima. You want to kick my (butt), bring it on."

Davis had scored six touchdowns against Notre Dame two years earlier, and the Irish hadn't kicked to him since. He pulled his kick-off team together and alerted them to expect a return.

The first kickoff sailed out of bounds. After a five-yard penalty, the next kickoff came end over end to Davis.

"I hadn't seen one in two years," he said.

There was a key block from Ricky Bell and another from Mosi Tatupu in the wedge. He started left and ran down the sideline right in front of Notre Dame coach Ara Parseghian.

"That's the only time collegiately or professionally, that I felt a crowd," he said. "It was like running through butter.

"It was like me running through something, the vibrations were that strong. They were actually hitting my body."

The touchdown electrified the Coliseum crowd of 83,552. If at the half the Trojans doubted their ability to come back against the Fighting Irish, they had a sideline of believers now.

Something almost otherworldly was about to unfold.

"I was the match to the wood," Davis said. "I lit the inferno. It was crazy."

Big play followed big play. A crushing tackle by David Lewis on the ensuing kickoff. A 6-yard scoring run by Davis. A fumble recovery led to a Davis 4-yard run and a USC lead, but things weren't about to ebb.

"It was the damnedest thing I ever saw in football," McKay said 20 years later. "I've never seen anything like it. Every time we got the ball, we scored. I don't know why every time we got the ball we scored. I'm sure some of my assistants understand why we scored. But I never did.

"I remember telling the coaches up in the press box, 'Come on down and witness this thing. I don't know what the hell's going on. I think it's pretty good.'"

The floodgates were open, and there was nothing Notre Dame could do. Haden threw two TDs to McKay's son, J.K. McKay, and another to Diggs. Charles Phillips intercepted two passes, one for a touchdown.

USC scored 55 points in less than 17 minutes.

"It was like they played on Saturday, and we came back on Sunday with whole other guys," Davis said. "It was crazy."

Davis played on two national championship teams at USC. He went on to play in the NFL, the WFL, the CFL and the USFL.

Yet he is forever identified from that Saturday afternoon, a day he rushed for only 56 yards from scrimmage, a day that altered his life forever. Starred in a game now spoken of in reverent terms.

"I didn't have a true perspective of the game until I got out of football, and then realized how it affected people," Davis said. "I knew it was dramatic, but the way people talk about it now, they consider it phenomenal.

"I figured, 'Well, somebody's going to do something the same way I did.' I remember talking to a reporter years ago and asking him why reporters keep calling me about that day. And he said, 'When somebody else duplicates that performance, then we'll stop talking to you.'"

USC plans to honor Davis on Saturday during the halftime of this year's Notre Dame game. He realizes now he will always be USC's Notre Dame killer, and that's OK, too.

If that day had never happened?

"I would just be a guy who went to a great school and played in a great rivalry, and that would have been it," he said. "I would have faded into oblivion."

Instead, fame from that game has helped him become partners in Jewelry by Arsa, a downtown store that manufactures diamond "USC No. 1" jewelry. It helped him launch his own clothing line, "A.D. 28."

And it left him with a lifetime of glory.

"It's been great for me," he said. "How many athletes can be talked to for 30 years about something they did? Some guys have long careers, they're walking around, and you don't even know who they are."

Staff photo by David Sprague

Trojans See Orange

BY SCOTT WOLF, *STAFF WRITER*

It took 11 games, but USC coach Pete Carroll finally mentioned the unmentionable to his team Saturday night.

"Let's go to the Rose Bowl (next week), win that game, too, and then let's go to the Orange Bowl," Carroll said, in his first utterance of the national championship game.

It's close enough to think about, especially after the top-ranked Trojans routed Notre Dame 41-10 before 92,611 rain-soaked fans at the Coliseum.

After stubbornly avoiding any talk about the Orange Bowl, Carroll stunned his players with his postgame comment alluding to the postseason situation.

"He doesn't really talk about it, so if he mentioned it, it means it must be coming," wide receiver Dwayne Jarrett said.

"Definitely, I was surprised," offensive lineman Sam Baker added.

With a victory over UCLA next week at the Rose Bowl, the Trojans will advance to the Orange Bowl on January 4, but first they made a little history, defeating the Irish by 31 points for the third successive year.

USC has never routed Notre Dame in three consecutive games, an accomplishment that was not lost on the seniors, who were playing in their final home game.

"I wouldn't have believed it before, and I'm part of those teams that beat Notre Dame by that much," linebacker Matt Grootegoed said.

The third victory was so matter of fact that there weren't any postgame scenes of fans rushing the field, although several seniors took their time walking off the Coliseum turf for the last time.

Another record fell as the Trojans won their 21st successive home game, breaking a school record set twice in the 1920s.

"To not lose in 21 straight games is phenomenal," tight end Alex Holmes said. "I think USC is back to what it was in the '70s."

The Trojans might be back to where they were in 2002, when quarterback Carson Palmer won the Heisman Trophy. Junior Matt Leinart, who had not thrown for more than 300 yards this season, passed for 400 and completed 24 of 34 passes with five touchdowns.

"I sure hope (he wins)," offensive coordinator Norm Chow said. "He's leading the best team in the country."

During the team's bus ride from the hotel to the Coliseum before the game, Leinart wondered if he would enjoy a big day, watching the rain pouring down in Los Angeles.

"You do kind of think about it, because the rain can do a lot," Leinart said.

And, initially, a few of his balls sailed (sometimes through the hands of Irish defenders) as Notre Dame took an early 10-3 lead.

It turned out to be just another typical slow start for the Trojans (11-0), who scored 38 successive points against a stubborn Irish defense that was impressive holding USC to 83 yards rushing.

LEFT: Steve Smith (2) fights off Notre Dame's Quentin Burrell after making a big first-half catch.
Staff photo by Hans Gutknecht

	1	2	3	4	Score
Notre Dame	7	3	0	0	10
USC	3	14	10	14	41

Scoring Summary

ND - Palmer 1-yard pass from Quinn (Fitzpatrick kick), 13 plays, 92 yards in 6:24

USC - Killeen 39-yard field goal, 11 plays, 46 yards in 4:58

ND - Fitzpatrick 28-yard field goal, 12 plays, 73 yards in 4:35

USC - Jarrett 12-yard pass from Leinart (Killeen kick), seven plays, 80 yards in 2:39

USC - Jarrett 57-yard pass from Leinart (Killeen kick), four plays, 73 yards in 1:55

USC - Killeen 42-yard field goal, 11 plays, 49 yards in 3:33

USC - Bush 69-yard pass from Leinart (Killeen kick), three plays, 78 yards in 1:38

USC - Smith 35-yard pass from Leinart (Killeen kick), six plays, 67 yards in 2:41

USC - Mitchell 23-yard pass from Leinart (Killeen kick), seven plays, 79 yards in 3:43

Team Statistics

	ND	USC
First Downs	16	23
Rushes-Yards (Net)	37-195	28-83
Passing Yards (Net)	105	405
Passes Att-Comp-Int	30-15-0	35-25-0
Total Offense Plays-Yards	67-300	63-488
Punt Returns-Yards	1-9	0-0
Kickoff Returns-Yards	5-106	2-26
Punts (Number-Avg)	8-43.9	3-35.7
Fumbles-Lost	2-0	1-0
Penalties-Yards	3-36	2-10
Possession Time	31:30	28:30
Sacks By (Number-Yards)	1-3	3-13

Individual Offensive Statistics

Rushing: **Notre Dame**-Grant 15-94; Walker 11-64; Quinn 8-30; Wilson 1-5; Thomas 1-2; Holiday 1-0.
USC-White 14-51; Bush 8-25; Leinart 3-7; Reed 1-2; Team 1-(-1); Dennis 1-(-1).

Passing: **Notre Dame**-Quinn 15-29-0-105; Holiday 0-1-0-0.
USC-Leinart 24-34-0-400; Cassel 1-1-0-5.

Receiving: **Notre Dame**-Walker 3-10; Fasano 2-25; Wilson 2-17; Shelton 2-13; Collins 2-9; Stovall 1-17; McKnight 1-9; Holiday 1-4; Palmer 1-1.
USC-Jarrett 6-102; Smith 4-96; Holmes 4-44; Byrd 4-23; Mitchell 2-38; Bush 1-69; McFoy 1-18; Webb 1-8; Buchanon 1-5; Kirtman 1-2.

Individual Defensive Statistics

Interceptions: **Notre Dame**-None.
USC-None.

Sacks (Unassisted-Assisted): **Notre Dame**-Budinscak 1-0.
USC-Team 1-0; Jackson 1-0; Sartz 1-0.

Tackles (Unassisted-Assisted): **Notre Dame**-Tuck 5-0; Burrell 5-0; Goolsby 5-0; Hoyte 3-2; Zbikowski 2-3; Curry 4-0; Jackson 3-0; Budinscak 2-1; Parish IV 2-1; Richardson 2-0; Landri 2-0.
USC-Tatupu 6-2; Grootegoed 5-1; Cody 4-2; Bing 5-0; Jackson 4-1; Wyatt 4-0; Wright 3-1; Sartz 3-1; Williams 3-0; Rucker 3-0; Patterson 3-0.

By stopping the run, the Irish (6-5) gave up the pass, with their zone coverages allowing USC's wide receivers to roam freely. On some

ABOVE: Dwayne Jarrett points to the fans after scoring USC's first TD of the game, one of five Matt Leinart touchdown passes. *Staff photo by Hans Gutknecht*

passes, two USC receivers were almost fighting for the ball, both were so open.

"Jason Mitchell stole my touchdown," wide receiver Steve Smith joked.

Smith caught four passes for 96 yards, including a 35-yard touchdown, in his first game back since breaking his leg against California in early October.

"I think I was killing them with the routes," Smith said. "I don't think they played anyone with our schemes."

With a 57-yard touchdown pass to Jarrett and 69-yard touchdown pass to Bush, Leinart put up the gaudy numbers that Heisman voters expect.

"It feels good to get a big game and get a lot of yards," Leinart said. "But I was just throwing passes, and guys were running with it."

Jarrett caught six passes for 102 yards despite Notre Dame's concerted effort to stop him with double-coverage.

"They came in trying to take Dwayne away," wide receivers coach Lane Kiffin said. "They really banged him around."

If Notre Dame's defense had done a better job stopping the pass, the game might have been more interesting. As it was, the Irish were down just 17-10 at halftime and trailed 20-10 when kicker D.J. Fitzpatrick missed a 39-yard field goal. Right after that, Bush broke free on his 69-yard touchdown, catching a short pass and sprinting down the sideline.

That sequence overshadowed Notre Dame's running game, which was good for 195 yards as USC's normally stingy run defense surrendered yardage at an unaccustomed rate.

After Bush's touchdown gave USC a 27-10 lead, the game became a typical blowout.

Carroll might have lost the moral high ground with Oklahoma coach Bob Stoops when he faked a punt with a 34-10 lead in the fourth quarter.

Notre Dame was called for pass interference on the play,

and Leinart quickly threw his fifth touchdown to close out the scoring.

"Was the fake punt inappropriate? No way," Notre Dame coach Tyrone Willingham said. "We play the game of football, and that is part of it."

BELOW: USC players give coach Pete Carroll a bath to celebrate their big victory over rival Notre Dame. *Staff photo by Hans Gutknecht*

This Year's Rivalry Brings Higher Stakes

BY RICH HAMMOND, *STAFF WRITER*

USC's goals are far loftier, but UCLA's are no less urgent. While the Trojans will have the national championship and the Heisman Trophy on their minds, the Bruins simply will be battling for respectability when the crosstown rivals meet Saturday at the Rose Bowl.

Every year during USC-UCLA week, the city is divided between red and blue, like a living version of that presidential electoral map.

Perhaps not since the 1960s has the game meant so much to both teams. A victory for either would have implications that would last long beyond the weekend.

For USC, the motivations are quite clear. A victory for the Trojans almost certainly would put them in the Orange Bowl, the Bowl Championship Series title game, on January 4 for a chance at a second consecutive national championship, something USC has not accomplished since 1931-32.

The Trojans maintained a healthy lead in both polls over Oklahoma and Auburn, neither of whom played over the week, and should maintain their lead when BCS standings are released today.

Nothing is certain, as the Trojans learned last year, but if the Trojans beat the rival Bruins by any margin, it's hard to imagine them being overtaken by Oklahoma, which faces a mediocre Colorado team in the Big 12 title game, or Auburn, which plays Tennessee in the SEC title game.

First, the Trojans must get past a UCLA team that will be motivated to end a six-game losing streak to USC and can play itself into a more lucrative bowl with a victory Saturday. The Pac-10 Conference has five bowl-eligible teams—USC (7-0 in conference), Cal (7-1), Arizona State (5-3), Oregon State (5-3) and UCLA (4-3)—and, regardless of what happens this weekend, all five teams will receive bowl bids.

USC is guaranteed a spot in the Orange Bowl or the Rose Bowl, but the situation is far murkier for UCLA, and much depends on Cal's game against Southern Mississippi and the whims of a few computers.

UCLA assured itself a bowl game with last week's victory over Oregon, but the Bruins' destination remains unknown. A UCLA win would put the Bruins in a three-way tie for third place with Arizona State and Oregon State, but it is likely that the Bruins would be chosen ahead of either of those teams.

The least likely assignment for the Bruins is the Sun Bowl (December 31 in El Paso, Texas) against Purdue. That would require a victory over USC plus a loss (or a fall from the No. 4 spot in the BCS) by Cal.

Staff photo by Michael Owen Baker

If Cal makes a BCS bowl and UCLA wins, the Bruins likely would go to the Holiday Bowl (December 30 in San Diego) and face a Big 12 team, with Texas A&M the probable pick at this point.

A UCLA loss doesn't necessarily clear things up. If the Bruins lose and Cal is selected to a BCS bowl, UCLA is certain to play in the Insight Bowl (December 26 in Phoenix) against Notre Dame.

Confused yet? There's one more. If UCLA loses and Cal doesn't make a BCS bowl, Cal would drop to the Holiday Bowl, Arizona State to the Sun Bowl, Oregon State to the Insight Bowl and UCLA would play in the Las Vegas Bowl (December 23) against a Mountain West Conference team, likely New Mexico.

It's not all about bowls for the Bruins. This is coach Karl Dorrell's second season. By this point of his second year, Pete Carroll had the Trojans rolling toward the Orange Bowl, and his coaching staff had turned Carson Palmer from an underachieving quarterback into a Heisman Trophy winner.

A victory over the Trojans would be the sort of eye-opener that would boost Dorrell's stature and quiet the grumbling of fans and boosters who already are thinking about Dorrell's possible replacements, although he signed a six-year contract that will take him through 2008.

Things are much simpler at USC, and it's not much of an exaggeration to say that the two programs are operating in different universes these days.

Matt Leinart's 400-yard, five-touchdown effort Saturday against Notre Dame might have moved him ahead of Oklahoma's Adrian Peterson and Jason White into the role of Heisman Trophy favorite.

If Leinart can duplicate his numbers from last year against UCLA, when he completed 23 of 32 attempts for 289 yards and two touchdowns, all in little more than three quarters of work, he will boost his Heisman chances. But UCLA has been far better on pass defense than run defense this year.

Either way, Leinart almost certainly has earned a plane ticket to New York for the Heisman ceremony. On Saturday, UCLA will try to deny him the hardware and will finally find out their postseason destination.

Staff photo by Michael Owen Baker

Clockwork Orange

BY SCOTT WOLF, *STAFF WRITER*

PASADENA—Virtually alone at his locker stall, Pete Carroll put on a crisp blue shirt as he got ready to leave the Rose Bowl on Saturday night.

"It's the only blue shirt I own," Carroll said.

There are no coincidences in Carroll's life, and breaking out a blue shirt wasn't one either, although it might have been worn more as a sign of respect than laughter following top-ranked USC's not-what-it-expected 29-24 victory over UCLA in front of 88,442.

Carroll certainly wasn't worried about the future because he knew the Trojans were headed to the Orange Bowl and the national championship game. Maybe that's because Orange Bowl officials passed out patches to USC players to sew onto their jerseys for the January 4 game.

"We've told them unofficially they'll be in our game," said Keith Tribble, chief executive officer of the Orange Bowl. "They started No. 1 and won every game. I expect them to be there."

It's considered a foregone conclusion, according to BCS analyst Jerry Palm.

"USC is fine. The Orange Bowl is set with USC and Oklahoma," Palm said. "USC is so far ahead, there would have to be a complete (poll) voter rebellion."

Even the normally cautious Carroll expressed his true feelings after the Trojans' sixth consecutive victory over the Bruins.

"It would be kind of nice to go to an Orange Bowl after what happened last year," Carroll said. "If it doesn't work out, I'm seceding from the union."

The Trojans (12-0) will play No. 2 Oklahoma, but for a few tenuous moments Saturday, they wondered whether they were headed to Miami after being pushed to the edge by the Bruins (6-5). It didn't matter that USC staggered into the championship game instead of waltzing.

"This last game in itself is an experience," Carroll said. "I learned that last year. There's a lot going on when you have to win the last game. The pressure is more obvious. I think we got outplayed in the second half. It was a great day for the rivalry."

Thanks to a dazzling effort by USC tailback Reggie Bush, who broke off Heisman-worthy touchdown runs of 65 and 81 yards, the Trojans cruised to a 20-10 halftime lead. But the Bruins came back and cut the lead to 23-17 with 1:35 left in the third quarter on a nine-yard run by Manuel White.

"At 23-17, that was a little hairy for us," Carroll said.

Ryan Killeen kicked his fifth field goal of the game to give the Trojans a 29-17 advantage with 3:49 remaining, but the Bruins scored again on a 4-yard reception by Marcedes Lewis with 2:20 left.

LEFT: Reggie Bush does a flip in to the end zone on a long TD in the first quarter against UCLA.
Staff photo by Hans Gutknecht

	1	2	3	4	Total
USC	10	10	3	6	29
UCLA	0	10	7	7	24

Scoring Summary
USC - Bush 65-yard run (Killeen kick), two plays, 67 yards in 0:58
USC - Killeen 37-yard field goal, 13 plays, 78 yards in 6:15
UCLA - Bragg 96-yard punt return (Medlock kick)
USC - Bush 81-yard run (Killeen kick), two plays, 78 yards in 0:37
UCLA - Medlock 43-yard field goal, eight plays, 62 yards in 3:13
USC - Killeen 42-yard field goal, five plays, 15 yards in 2:41
USC - Killeen 34-yard field goal, five plays, 39 yards in 1:21
UCLA - White 9-yard run (Medlock kick), seven plays, 81 yards in 1:49
USC - Killeen 36-yard field goal, 11 plays, 51 yards in 4:30
USC - Killeen 34-yard field goal, four plays, four yards in 2:22
UCLA - Lewis 4-yard pass from Olson (Medlock kick), seven plays, 80 yards in 1:29

Team Statistics
	USC	UCLA
First downs	19	12
Rushes-Yards (Net)	37-235	25-17
Passing Yards (Net)	242	278
Passes Att-Comp-Int	34-24-1	34-20-2
Total Offense Plays-Yards	71-477	59-295
Punt Returns-Yards	3-25	3-102
Kickoff Returns-Yards	3-88	4-113
Punts (Number-Avg)	5-36.0	7-43.9
Fumbles-Lost	2-1	2-1
Penalties-Yards	4-40	5-35
Time of Possession	34:33	25:27
Sacks By (Number-Yards)	3-13	3-24

Individual Offensive Statistics
Rushing: **USC**-Bush 15-204, L.White 16-75, team 2-(-5), Malone 1-(-15), Leinart 3-(-24).
UCLA-M.White 7-13, Walker 1-11, Markey 8-5, Pitre 1-4, Breazell 2-3, Drew 2-(-5), Olson 4-(-14).

Passing: **USC**-Leinart 24-34-1-242.
UCLA-Olson 20-34-2-278.

Receiving: **USC**-Bush 6-73, Jarrett 5-44, S.Smith 4-37, Mitchell 2-36, L.White 2-13, Byrd 2-8, Holmes 1-21, Kirtman 1-7, Webb 1-3.
UCLA-Bragg 6-67, Taylor 5-89, Lewis 4-29, Perry 3-78, M.White 1-11, Pitre 1-4.

Individual Defensive Statistics:
Interceptions: **USC**-Tatupu 1-4; Leach 1-6.
UCLA-London 1-4.

Sacks: **USC**-Wright 1.0; Cody 1.0; Rucker 1.0
UCLA-Brown 2.0; Clark 1.0.

Tackles (Unassisted-Assisted): **USC**-Tatupu 8-2; Wright 4-1; Leach 4-1; Bing 4-1; Wyatt 3-1; Patterson 2-2; Cody 2-1; Jackson 2-0; Rucker 2-0; Grootegoed 2-0.
UCLA-T. Brown 7-1; London 6-2; Clark 6-2; Havner 4-2; Page 4-2; K. Brown 3-1; Niusulu 1-3; Harwell 3-0; McNeal 3-0; Walker 3-0; Emanuel 2-1; Team 2-0; Lorier 2-0; Morgan 2-0.

Bush fumbled (for the seventh consecutive game) with 53 seconds left at the Bruins' 15-yard line, but quarterback Drew Olson's next pass was intercepted by USC safety Jason Leach to put the game away.

Just like so many other games, the Trojans said they never panicked.

"It wasn't an easy win," linebacker Matt Grootegoed said. "We thought we had them, but it was emotionally draining. Our special teams struggled, our offense sputtered, we gave up some yards on defense. We didn't play our best game. But we came out ahead."

It's all literally a game for Carroll, who relished his first close encounter with the Bruins in four meetings. The first three were won by an average of 25 points.

"I like games like this," Carroll said. "There's so much more coaching going on. There's so many more decisions. We were in control the whole time. I felt in control. We did what championship teams had to do."

Carroll even shook his head and smiled after UCLA completed a 39-yard pass on its final touchdown drive.

"We made it so dramatic," Carroll said. "We wanted to get that done right there. It was fitting we finished on defense (on Leach's interception)."

The Trojans controlled most of the game, with little thanks to the offense in the second half. Quarterback Matt Leinart did not throw a touchdown pass for the first time as a starter (25 games), and the receivers dropped several easy catches.

"Yeah, I'm frustrated," USC offensive coordinator Norm Chow said. "I don't know what the problem was. We dropped passes, we fumbled the ball."

If Leinart shined against Notre Dame, he was just average against UCLA.

"I was a little out of rhythm at times because they were bringing pressure," said Leinart, who was sacked three times.

USC's usual second-half rout never materialized.

"The second half we usually reign and we didn't this time, but we played the way we had to," center Ryan Kalil said.

A four-point loss sounded like a moral victory, but UCLA wasn't satisfied with the outcome.

"It felt like we could have won this game," UCLA safety Jarrad Page said. "That's what's so disappointing. It hurts way more (than the last two)."

BELOW: Kicker Ryan Killeen (16) is congratulated by quarterback Matt Leinart after kicking a field goal in the fourth quarter. *Staff photo by Michael Owen Baker*

RIGHT: Matt Cassel (10) goes up high to recover an on-side kick at the end of the fourth quarter against UCLA. *Staff photo by Hans Gutknecht*

One More Mess for BCS

BY KEVIN MODESTI, *STAFF WRITER*

Well, there's another fine season spoiled by the Bowl Championship Series, the fingernail on the chalkboard in every university classroom in the land.

USC's players and coaches are the lucky ones, their undisputed No. 1 ranking giving them an argument-free trip to the Orange Bowl national-title game against Oklahoma and the pleasure of not having every conversation stained by the syllables "BCS."

Below the Trojans in the final rankings announced Sunday, it's a purgatory of BCS politics and arithmetic for frustrated Auburn and angry Cal and almost every good team to some extent.

You want the three little syllables that college football is supposed to be all about? Hold That Line. Block That Kick. Fourth And One. Go For It. Sis-Boom-Bah. Cold Beer Here. Fire The Coach. Go Big Red. Knute Rockne. Tom Harmon. New Year's Day. The Rose Bowl.

Not "BCS."

College-football-stadium buzz is supposed to be about big-hearted coaches and heady quarterbacks and water-bug tailbacks and hard-hitting linebackers and ice-veined kickers.

Not cynical conjecture about the biases of the BCS ranking formula.

Sunday was supposed to be about celebrating the best teams of the just-ended regular season and looking forward to their bowl-game rewards. Not insincere smiles from schools whose hopes were crushed by the BCS's confusing combination of human judgment and computer ratings.

Unfortunately, every day of this great season . . . while USC and Oklahoma and Auburn and two smaller outfits were rolling up undefeated records . . . while more players were putting together Heisman Trophy-caliber performances than you can count on the statue's extended right hand . . . the radio waves and the newspaper pages were dominated by mind-numbing analysis of the BCS standings.

Is it just me, because I'm in the words business, or does it grate on everybody that "BCS" looms larger in the language of football these days than "bump and run"?

Whatever system college football eventually settles on for choosing its national champion—and eventually it will be dragged kicking and screaming to a playoff system—should be judged by the same standard as the referee and the field condition and any such necessary evil.

You'll know it's OK when you don't have to talk about it. That certainly cannot be said of the BCS in its various forms since its 1998 debut.

Auburn, despite a 12-0 record, is stuck at No. 3 and relegated to the January 3 Sugar

Staff photo by Andy Holzman

Bowl against No. 8 Virginia Tech without a shot at the official national title. The Tigers have an even better gripe than the Trojans did last year when they were left out of the title game with a one-loss record.

Cal, 10-1 with its only loss to USC, was dropped from No. 4 to No. 5 after a closer-than-expected victory Saturday over Southern Mississippi and will settle for the December 30 Holiday Bowl against Texas Tech instead of the January 1 Rose Bowl. The Golden Bears have a right to be disappointed.

Trojans coach Pete Carroll was speaking with reporters on campus after Sunday's bowl-matchups announcement when Cal coach Jeff Tedford appeared on a television screen.

"If you have to go in and blow people out," said Tedford, who passed up an attempt to widen Cal's 26-16 edge on Southern Miss, "I don't think that's good for the integrity of the game."

Carroll seemed to agree.

"The issue of how they fell down (in the rankings) when they continued to win and play good football," Carroll said of the Golden Bears, "needs to be looked into."

BCS directors thought they'd improved the formula by increasing the influence of the writers' and coaches' polls. They didn't account for the possibility that—for the first time in the system's seven seasons—there would be more than two major undefeated teams.

Now people who used to hold their tongues about the ugliness of it all have stripped off the gloves.

"I wasn't going to gripe about the system last year," said Carroll, whose 2003 Trojans will be remembered as unofficial "co-champions" with LSU. "I'm not going to praise it this year because we came out on top. It's a system that's in the process of being perfected."

Staff photo by Evan Yee

After sorting out the four major bowl matchups Sunday, BCS coordinator Kevin Weiberg indicated a willingness to "take a look at" further tweaks in the rating formula, whether the system still encourages teams to run up scores on weak opponents (as Cal didn't), and whether coaches are flouting etiquette by vocally lobbying for poll support (as Texas' Mack Brown did).

Lucky for the Trojans they don't have to think about those things between now and the January 4 Orange Bowl in Miami. They're No. 1 in both human polls, just as they were a year ago, and this time that's good enough to make them No. 1 in the rankings that determine the national-championship pairing.

Now they don't have to worry about anything more complicated than running, passing, blocking, tackling and kicking and beating No. 2 for the title.

For a while, here, it'll almost feel like college football again.

It's Unanimous: USC Captures Title in Rout

BY SCOTT WOLF, *STAFF WRITER*

Doug Pensinger/Getty Images

MIAMI—USC linebacker Matt Grootegoed looked up at the scoreboard in disbelief Tuesday night—and that was before halftime.

"It's pretty surprising to see that score with all the hype," Grootegoed said. "We expected it to be closer."

So did a lot of other people, but the greatest game ever was quickly overshadowed by one of USC's greatest halves ever, as the top-ranked Trojans resoundingly claimed the national title with a 55-19 rout of second-ranked Oklahoma in the Orange Bowl in front of 77,912 at Pro Player Stadium.

The Trojans scored 38 points in the first half to easily put the game out of reach as Heisman Trophy winner Matt Leinart threw four touchdown passes. USC's 38-first-half points tied the most a Bob Stoops-led Oklahoma team ever allowed in an entire game.

"I'm speechless," receiver Dwayne Jarrett said moments after the Trojans won their second consecutive national title, but first undisputed championship since 1972.

Tailback LenDale White said: "We did surprise them. They know what happened tonight. They got their butt kicked."

The Trojans' 38 points in the half was a school record for a bowl game, eclipsing the 35 points USC scored in the second half of the 1973 Rose Bowl against Ohio State. Spectators began leaving at halftime as the Trojans built a 38-10 advantage.

"We didn't expect it to be this easy, but the game went our way from the beginning," USC coach Pete Carroll said. "We controlled all phases of the game."

Turnovers dictated the outcome as Oklahoma committed four in the first half, which led to 24 points for the Trojans. USC (13-0) did not have a turnover in the half as USC won its second title in two years for Carroll.

"They controlled the line of scrimmage," Oklahoma coach Bob Stoops said. "You can't make as many mistakes as we did and expect to win."

Unlike last year, when USC shared the national title with Louisiana State, the Trojans owned this one unanimously.

"This is a lot better," defensive end Frostee Rucker said. "We're not sharing anything. There's no questions asked. We're No. 1 and there's no doubts."

Defensive tackle Shaun Cody added: "Winning the game last year, we didn't know whether we would be champs or not. This year, we got the job done."

The game hardly lived up to its billing, with the Trojans spotting the Sooners a touchdown before scoring 28 consecutive points.

LEFT: Steve Smith (2) celebrates with teammate David Kirtman (37) after catching a 33-yard touchdown pass. *Jamie Squire/Getty Images*

	1st	2nd	3rd	4th	Final
Oklahoma	7	3	0	9	19
USC	14	24	10	7	55

Scoring Summary

OU - T.Wilson 5-yard pass from J.White (Hartley kick), 12 plays, 92 yards in 5:56

USC - Byrd 33-yard pass from Leinart (Killeen kick), six plays, 75 yards in 3:17

USC - White 6-yard run (Killeen kick), one play, six yards in :06

USC - Jarrett 54-yard pass from Leinart (Killeen kick), six plays, 89 yards in 1:41

USC - Smith 5-yard pass from Leinart (Killeen kick), 9:17. three plays, 10 yards in :49

OU - Hartley 29-yard field goal, 13 plays, 68 yards in 6:07

USC - Smith 33-yard pass from Leinart (Killeen kick), four plays, 79 yards in 1:14

USC - Killeen 44-yard field goal, seven plays, eight yards in :50.

USC - Smith 4-yard pass from Leinart (Killeen kick), eight plays, 85 yards in 3:07

USC - Killeen 42-yard field goal, nine plays, 45 yards in 2:34

USC - White 8-yard run (Killeen kick), five plays, 56 yards in 3:00

OU - Safety, Leinart downed in end zone

OU - T.Wilson 9-yard pass from J.White (Hartley kick), six plays, 49 yards in 2:35

Team Statistics

	OU	USC
First Downs	19	19
Rushes-Yards (Net)	40-128	28-193
Passing Yards (Net)	244	332
Pass Att-Comp-Int	36-24-3	35-18-0
Total Offense Plays-Yards	76-372	63-525
Punts Returns-Yards	1-3	1-7
Kickoff Returns-Yards	7-139	2-36
Punts (Number-Avg)	4-44.5	4-43.5
Fumbles-Lost	3-2	1-0
Penalties-Yards	3-30	9-75
Time Of Possession	35:06	24:54
Sacks by (Number-Yards)	1-9	2-20

Individual Offensive Statistics

Rushing: **OU**-Peterson 25-82; Wolfe 7-40; K.Jones 4-9; T.Wilson 1-5; J.White 3-(-8).
USC-White 15-118; Bush 6-75; Kirtman 1-4; Webb 1-4; Reed 2-2; Byrd 1-1; Leinart 2-(-11).

Passing: **OU**-J.White 24-36-3-244; Grady 0-0-0-0.
USC-Leinart 18-35-0-332; Cassel 0-0-0-0.

Receiving: **OU**-T.Wilson 7-59; Clayton 4-21; Bradley 2-66; K. Jones 2-30; B. Jones 2-13; Peterson 2-6; Rankins 2-0; Finley 1-23; Peoples 1-18; Moses 1-8.
USC-S.Smith 7-113; Jarrett 5-115; Byrd 3-58; Bush 2-31; Kirtman 1-15.

Individual Defensive Statistics

Interceptions: **OU**-None.
USC-E.Wright 1-22; Grootegoed 1-9; Leach 1-0.

Sacks (unassisted-assisted): **OU**-D. Cody 1-0.
USC-S. Cody 1-0; Tatupu 1-0.

Tackles (unassisted-assisted): **OU**-Pool 6-1; Nicholson 3-3; Mitchell 1-5; Alexander 2-3; Walker 2-3; Perkins 2-2; D.Cody 2-1; Ingram 2-1; McGruder 2-0; T. Wilson 2-0.
USC-Tatupu 7-5; Bing 5-5; Leach 5-2; Grootegoed 4-3; S.Cody 2-3; Rivers 3-1; E.Wright 3-1; Sartz 2-1; M.Wright 2-1; Tolliver 1-2; Patterson 0-3; Ting 0-3; Jackson 2-0; Rucker 2-0; Thomas 2-0.

ABOVE: **Steve Smith catches a 48-yard pass in the third quarter.** *Doug Pensinger/Getty Images*

A major reason for the lopsided score was USC's defense shutting down Oklahoma tailback Adrian Peterson, who was held to 82 yards on 25 carries.

"We had a month to prepare for him and shut him down," Rucker said. "We used our lateral speed."

Without Peterson posing problems, Oklahoma was forced to rely on quarterback Jason White, who threw three interceptions.

"They didn't do anything we didn't expect," White said. "They are just a great football team."

As usually happens when a team wins a national title, there are claims that no one expected it, even though the Trojans were a wire-to-wire No. 1 in the top 25 polls since August.

"I expected a blowout," USC linebacker Lofa Tatupu said. "But everyone else wrote us off."

The game turned almost in minutes as Oklahoma committed two inexcusable blunders.

With the game tied 7-7, USC's Tom Malone punted toward the goal line and as the ball bounced near the 3-yard line, Oklahoma's Mark Bradley inexplicably picked it up despite being surrounded by Trojans.

Bradley fumbled as he was hit by USC's Collin Ashton and safety Josh Pinkard recovered it the 6-yard line. On the next play,

RIGHT: **Steve Smith catches a 33-yard touchdown pass against Brodney Poole.** *Brian Bahr/Getty Images*

LenDale White, showing no signs of a sore ankle, scored the touchdown to put USC ahead 14-7.

"I don't know if it was the greatest decision for him to pick that ball up," Ashton said. "I was very surprised when he did it. I hit him and looked up and saw the ball pop up."

Pinkard was equally shocked, although the freshman remained cool enough to grab the loose ball.

"Hopefully, people will remember me," Pinkard said. "It didn't make any sense to me but I was happy to make something happen."

White then committed a major gaffe when he threw a ball up for grabs with five USC players surrounding one Oklahoma receiver, Mark Clayton. USC safety Jason Leach intercepted the pass at the Trojans' 11 and ended a potential scoring drive.

"They say the Pac-10 is not a strong conference, but I think Oklahoma was shocked we punched them in the mouth early," defensive end Lawrence Jackson said.

That sequence eliminated the suspense as Leinart connected on a 54-yard scoring pass to Jarrett that gave the Trojans a 21-7 advantage with 11:46 left in the half.

White then threw his second interception, which was returned to the Oklahoma 10 by cornerback Eric Wright. Three plays later, Leinart threw a 5-yard touchdown pass to receiver Steve Smith and USC was routing the Sooners 28-7.

Leinart was named the game's outstanding player, completing 18 of 35 passes for 332 yards and five touchdowns.

"I couldn't imagine this situation two or three years ago under Carson Palmer," Leinart said of the Heisman Trophy-winning quarterback he replaced at USC.

The Sooners finally stopped the slide when Garrett Hartley kicked a 29-yard field goal to make it 28-10 but it was too little, too late.

The Trojans immediately countered with a 45-yard run by Bush and Smith then cradled a 34-yard touchdown reception with one arm as Oklahoma safety Brodney Pool tugged at his arm to make it 35-10. It was Leinart's fourth touchdown pass, the seventh time in 26 starts he has thrown at least four touchdowns.

Leinart's four touchdown passes in a half were an Orange Bowl record.

Things got even worse for the Sooners as Ryan Killeen added a 44-yard field goal just before the half and Leinart threw a 4-yard touchdown pass to Smith in the third quarter to boost USC's lead to 45-10.

Oklahoma actually scored first as White calmly avoided USC's pass rush to find receivers on the Sooners' opening drive. White completed two third-and-8 situations on the drive, with USC cornerbacks falling down on both plays.

His first third-down conversion was a 20-yard pass to Travis Wilson as Kevin Arbet fell down. The second, a 32-yard completion to Bradley, occurred as Wright slipped and fell and Bradley went all the way to the USC 7-yard line.

White threaded a 5-yard touchdown pass to Wilson to give Oklahoma a 7-0 lead with 7:44 left in the first quarter.

But USC struck back immediately, as tight end Dominique Byrd made another highlight-reel, one-handed catch for a 33-yard touchdown that tied it 7-7. It was reminiscent of Byrd's one-handed grab against Oregon State.

"I knew this was the biggest stage of my career," Byrd said.

Leinart was 5 for 5 on the drive for 80 yards, with Byrd catching the final two for 50 yards.

RIGHT: Matt Leinart scrambles against the Oklahoma Sooners defense. *Brian Bahr/Getty Images*

LEFT: Jason White (18) of the Oklahoma Sooners reacts after throwing an interception.
Brian Bahr/Getty Images

BELOW: Head coach Pete Carroll is hit with the Gatorade bucket as the Orange Bowl comes to a close. *Brian Bahr/Getty Images*

LEFT: Steve Smith celebrates after catching a 5-yard touchdown pass against the Oklahoma Sooners in the second quarter.
Doug Pensinger/Getty Images

RIGHT: LenDale White of the USC Trojans holds the championship trophy like a football.
Doug Pensinger/Getty Images

ABOVE: Pete Carroll holds the sword he used to direct the band after defeating the Oklahoma Sooners 55-19 to win the FedEx Orange Bowl 2005 National Championship.
Doug Pensinger/Getty Images

USC TEAM STATISTICS

Category	USC	Opp.	Category	USC	Opp.	Category	USC	Opp.
Scoring	496	169	Average Per Game	271.7	199.9	Net Punt Average	38.5	38.6
Points Per Game	38.2	13.0	Touchdowns Passing	34	13	Time of Possession (Game)	31:43	28:17
First Downs	292	201	Total Offense	5838	3631	Third Down Conversions	79/182	54/190
Rushing	123	66	Total Plays	923	851	Third Down Percentage	43%	28%
Passing	150	124	Average Per Play	6.3	4.3	Fourth Down Conversions	11/21	10/19
Penalty	19	11	Average Per Game	449.1	279.3	Fourth Down Percentage	52%	53%
Rushing Yardage	2306	1032	Kick Returns (Number-Yards)	30-687	45-952	Sacks By-Yards	50-344	25-176
Yards gained rushing	2646	1561	Punt Returns (Number-Yards)	30-406	22-203	Miscellaneous Yards	32	4
Yards lost rushing	340	529	Int Returns (Number-Yards)	22-358	7-75	Touchdowns Scored	64	20
Rushing Attempts	493	394	Kick Return Average	22.9	21.2	Field Goal-Attempts	16-25	10-16
Average Per Rush	4.7	2.6	Punt Return Average	13.5	9.2	Extra Point Attempts	64-64	17-18
Average Per Game	177.4	79.4	Int Return Average	16.3	10.7	Attendance (Average)	85229	55838
Touchdowns Rushing	27	5	Fumbles-Lost	26-12	33-16			
Passing Yardage	3532	2599	Penalties-Yards	73-587	77-554			
Att-Comp-Int	430-282-7	457-246-22	Average Per Game	45.2	42.6			
Average Per Pass	8.2	5.7	Punts-Yards	51-2165	85-3691			
Average Per Catch	12.5	10.6	Average Per Punt	42.5	43.4			

Score by Quarters

Team	1st	2nd	3rd	4th	Total
USC	96	176	114	110	496
Opponents	33	71	39	26	169

INDIVIDUAL OFFENSIVE STATISTICS

RUSHING

Player	GP	Att	Gain	Loss	Net	Avg	TD	Long	Avg/g
LenDale White	13	203	1128	25	1103	5.4	15	54	84.8
Reggie Bush	13	143	971	63	908	6.3	6	81	69.8
Desmond Reed	13	31	182	9	173	5.6	1	28	13.3
Hershel Dennis	9	28	116	7	109	3.9	1	13	12.1
David Kirtman	13	8	45	0	45	5.6	0	14	3.5
Lee Webb	13	6	29	0	29	4.8	1	9	2.2
Matt Cassel	9	6	18	7	11	1.8	0	8	1.2
John Griffin	2	2	9	0	9	4.5	0	7	4.5
Andre Woodert	2	1	4	0	4	4.0	0	4	2.0
Dominique Bird	9	1	1	0	1	1.0	0	1	0.1
Steve Smith	8	1	0	1	-1	-1.0	0	0	-0.1
Brandon Hance	5	2	0	4	-4	-2.0	0	0	-0.8
Tom Malone	13	1	0	15	-15	-15.0	0	0	-1.2
Team	9	11	0	22	-22	-2.0	0	0	-2.4
Matt Leinart	13	49	143	187	-44	-0.9	3	23	-3.4
Total	**13**	**493**	**2646**	**340**	**2306**	**4.7**	**27**	**81**	**177.4**
Opponents	**13**	**394**	**1561**	**529**	**1032**	**2.6**	**5**	**82**	**79.4**

PASSING

Player	GP	Effic	Att-Comp-Int	Pct	Yds	TD	Long	Avg/G
Matt Leinart	13	156.54	412-269-6	65.3	3322	33	69	255.5
Matt Cassel	9	115.34	14-10-1	71.4	97	0	22	10.8
Brandon Hance	5	150.40	1-1-0	100.0	6	0	6	1.2
Reggie Bush	13	866.80	1-1-0	100.0	52	1	52	4.0
Team	9	0.00	1-0-0	0.0	0	0	0	0.0
Desmond Reed	13	562.00	1-1-0	100.0	55	0	55	4.2
Total	**13**	**157.42**	**430-282-7**	**65.6**	**3532**	**34**	**69**	**271.7**
Opponents	**13**	**101.36**	**457-246-22**	**53.8**	**2599**	**13**	**69**	**199.9**

RECEIVING

Player	GP	No.	Yds	Avg	TD	Long	Avg/G
Dwayne Jarrett	13	55	849	15.4	13	57	65.3
Reggie Bush	13	43	509	11.8	7	69	39.2
Steve Smith	8	42	660	15.7	6	51	82.5
Dominique Byrd	9	37	384	10.4	3	33	42.7
Alex Holmes	13	24	244	10.2	0	48	18.8
Chris McFoy	12	21	272	13.0	0	31	22.7
David Kirtman	13	19	161	8.5	1	26	12.4
Jason Mitchell	12	13	226	17.4	2	33	18.8
LenDale White	13	11	97	8.8	2	22	7.5
Lee Webb	13	4	47	11.8	0	22	3.6
Fred Davis	9	4	30	7.5	0	15	3.3
William Buchanon	12	4	15	3.8	0	6	1.2
Desmond Reed	13	3	0	0.0	0	2	0.0
John Walker	13	1	22	22.0	0	22	1.7
Jody Adewale	5	1	16	16.0	0	16	3.2
Total	**13**	**282**	**3532**	**12.5**	**34**	**69**	**271.7**
Opponents	**13**	**246**	**2599**	**10.6**	**13**	**69**	**199.9**

PUNT RETURNS

Player	No.	Yds	Avg	TD	Long
Reggie Bush	24	376	15.7	2	65
Greig Carlson	5	14	2.8	0	6
Desmond Reed	1	16	16.0	0	16
Total	**30**	**406**	**13.5**	**2**	**65**
Opponents	**22**	**203**	**9.2**	**1**	**96**

INTERCEPTIONS

Player	No.	Yds.	Avg.	TD	Long
Matt Grootegoed	5	107	21.4	0	57
Jason Leach	3	20	6.7	0	14
Lofa Tatupu	3	38	12.7	0	32
Darnell Bing	2	8	4.0	0	8
Eric Wright	2	22	11.0	0	22
Terrell Thomas	2	29	14.5	0	29
Dallas Sartz	1	8	8.0	0	8
Justin Wyatt	1	19	19.0	0	19
Keith Rivers	1	22	22.0	0	22
Lawrence Jackson	1	19	19.0	0	19
Kevin Arbet	1	66	66.0	0	66
Total	**22**	**358**	**16.3**	**0**	**66**
Opponents	**7**	**75**	**10.7**	**1**	**28**

KICK RETURNS

Player	No.	Yds	Avg	TD	Long
Reggie Bush	21	537	25.6	0	84
Desmond Reed	7	150	21.4	0	49
Josh Pinkard	1	0	0.0	0	0
Hershel Dennis	1	0	0.0	0	0
Total	**30**	**687**	**22.9**	**0**	**84**
Opponents	**45**	**952**	**21.2**	**0**	**54**

FUMBLE RETURNS

Player	No.	Yds	Avg	TD	Long
Lofa Tatupu	1	12	12.0	0	12
Manuel Wright	1	20	20.0	1	20
Total	**2**	**32**	**16.0**	**1**	**20**
Opponents	**1**	**4**	**4.0**	**0**	**4**

SCORING

Player	TD	FGs	Kick	Rush	Rcv	Pass	DXP	Saf	Points
Ryan Killeen	0	16-25	64-64	0-0	0	0-0	0	0	112
LenDale White	17	0-0	0-0	0-0	0	0-0	0	0	102
Reggie Bush	15	0-0	0-0	0-0	0	0-0	0	0	90
Dwayne Jarrett	13	0-0	0-0	0-0	0	0-0	0	0	78
Steve Smith	6	0-0	0-0	0-0	0	0-0	0	0	36
Dominique Byrd	3	0-0	0-0	0-0	0	0-0	0	0	18
Matt Leinart	3	0-0	0-0	0-0	0	0-0	0	0	18
Jason Mitchell	2	0-0	0-0	0-0	0	0-0	0	0	12
Hershel Dennis	1	0-0	0-0	0-0	0	0-0	0	0	6
David Kirtman	1	0-0	0-0	0-0	0	0-0	0	0	6
Desmond Reed	1	0-0	0-0	0-0	0	0-0	0	0	6
Lee Webb	1	0-0	0-0	0-0	0	0-0	0	0	6
Manuel Wright	1	0-0	0-0	0-0	0	0-0	0	0	6
Total	**64**	**16-25**	**64-64**	**0-0**	**0**	**0-0**	**0**	**0**	**496**
Opponents	**20**	**10-16**	**17-18**	**0-0**	**0**	**0-2**	**0**	**1**	**169**

TOTAL OFFENSE

Player	G	Plays	Rush	Pass	Total	Avg/G
Matt Leinart	13	461	-44	3322	3278	252.2
LenDale White	13	203	1103	0	1103	84.8
Reggie Bush	13	144	908	52	960	73.8
Desmond Reed	13	32	173	55	228	17.5
Hershel Dennis	9	28	109	0	109	12.1
Matt Cassel	9	20	11	97	108	12.0
David Kirtman	13	8	45	0	45	3.5
Lee Webb	13	6	29	0	29	2.2
John Griffin	2	2	9	0	9	4.5
Andre Woodert	2	1	4	0	4	2.0
Brandon Hance	5	3	-4	6	2	0.4
Dominique Byrd	9	1	1	0	1	0.1
Steve Smith	8	1	-1	0	-1	-0.1
Tom Malone	13	1	-15	0	-15	-1.2
Team	9	12	-22	0	-22	-2.4
Total	**13**	**923**	**2306**	**3532**	**5838**	**449.1**
Opponents	**13**	**851**	**1032**	**2599**	**3631**	**279.3**

FIELD GOALS

Player	FGM-FGA	Pct	01-19	20-29	30-39	40-49	50-99	Long	Blkd
Ryan Killeen	16-25	64.0	0-0	2-4	8-10	6-11	0-0	44	1

PUNTING

Player	No.	Yds	Avg	Long	TB	FC	I20	Blkd
Tom Malone	49	2144	43.8	62	10	7	20	1
Team	2	21	10.5	21	0	0	0	1
Total	**51**	**2165**	**42.5**	**62**	**10**	**7**	**20**	**2**
Opponents	**85**	**3691**	**43.4**	**79**	**2**	**18**	**19**	**0**

ALL PURPOSE

Player	G	Rush	Rec	PR	KOR	IR	Total	Avg/G
Reggie Bush	13	908	509	376	537	0	2330	179.2
LenDale White	13	1103	97	0	0	0	1200	92.3
Dwayne Jarrett	13	0	849	0	0	0	849	65.3
Steve Smith	13	-1	660	0	0	0	659	82.4
Dominique Byrd	9	1	384	0	0	0	385	42.8
Desmond Reed	13	173	0	16	150	0	339	26.1
Chris McFoy	12	0	272	0	0	0	272	22.7
Alex Holmes	13	0	244	0	0	0	244	18.8
Jason Mitchell	12	0	226	0	0	0	226	18.8
David Kirtman	13	45	161	0	0	0	206	15.8
Hershel Dennis	9	109	0	0	0	0	109	12.1
Matt Grootegoed	13	0	0	0	0	107	107	8.2
Lee Webb	13	29	47	0	0	0	76	5.8
Kevin Arbet	12	0	0	0	0	66	66	5.5
Lofa Tatupu	13	0	0	0	0	38	38	2.9
Fred Davis	9	0	30	0	0	0	30	3.3
Terrell Thomas	11	0	0	0	0	29	29	2.6
Keith Rivers	13	0	0	0	0	22	22	1.7
John Walker	13	0	22	0	0	0	22	1.7
Eric Wright	13	0	0	0	0	22	22	1.7
Jason Leach	13	0	0	0	0	20	20	1.5
Lawrence Jackson	13	0	0	0	0	19	19	1.5
Justin Wyatt	13	0	0	0	0	19	19	1.5
Jody Adewale	5	0	16	0	0	0	16	3.2
William Buchanon	12	0	15	0	0	0	15	1.2
Greig Carlson	11	0	0	14	0	0	14	1.3
Matt Cassel	9	11	0	0	0	0	11	1.2
John Griffin	2	9	0	0	0	0	9	4.5
Dallas Sartz	13	0	0	0	0	8	8	0.6
Darnell Bing	12	0	0	0	0	8	8	0.7
Andre Woodert	2	4	0	0	0	0	4	2.0
Brandon Hance	5	-4	0	0	0	0	-4	-0.8
Tom Malone	13	-15	0	0	0	0	-15	-1.2
Team	9	-22	0	0	0	0	-22	-2.4
Matt Leinart	13	-44	0	0	0	0	-44	-3.4
Total	**13**	**2306**	**3532**	**406**	**687**	**358**	**7289**	**560.7**
Opponents	**13**	**1032**	**2599**	**203**	**952**	**75**	**4861**	**373.9**

INDIVIDUAL DEFENSIVE STATISTICS

Player	GP	Solo	Ast	Total	TFl-Yds	No-Yds	Int-Yds	BrUp	QBH	Rcv-Yds	FF	Blkd Kick	Saf
Lofa Tatupu	13	57	47	104	13.5-43	6.0-28	3-38	8	.	2-12	3	.	.
Matt Grootegoed	13	42	26	68	12.5-46	3.0-24	5-107	4	1	2-0	1	.	.
Darnell Bing	12	43	20	63	8.0-22	0.5-5	2-87	.	.	2	.	.	.
Jason Leach	13	38	13	51	1.0-2	.	3-20	4	1	1-0	1	.	.
Dallas Sartz	13	22	26	48	3.5-11	1.5-5	1-8	6	.	.	1	.	.
Mike Patterson	13	24	21	45	15.5-72	5.5-35	.	2	1	4-0	2	.	.
Shaun Cody	13	29	16	45	13.0-96	10.0-88	.	3	5	.	2	1	.
Justin Wyatt	13	34	7	41	5.0-10	0.5-4	1-19	7	.	.	1	.	.
Eric Wright	13	27	6	33	2.0-13	2.0-13	2-22	6	.	1-0	.	.	.
Lawrence Jackson	13	19	13	32	11.0-41	6.0-31	1-19	1	.	.	.	.	.
Frostee Rucker	13	21	8	29	7.5-32	2.5-15	.	2	.	1-0	1	.	.
Kevin Arbet	12	19	7	26	0.5-0	.	1-66	2	1	.	.	.	.
Keith Rivers	13	13	12	25	3.0-23	2.5-2	21-22	1	.	.	1	.	.
Manuel Wright	11	11	12	23	6.0-17	2.0-10	.	2	.	2-20	.	.	.
Ronald Nunn	10	10	9	19	1.5-9	1.0-9	.	.	.	1-0	1	.	.
Jeff Schweiger	12	7	11	18	4.5-32	2.0-27	.	1	.	.	1	.	.
Collin Ashton	13	9	7	16	1.0-5	1.0-5	.	.	.	.	1	.	.
Scott Ware	7	9	7	16	.	.	.	1	.	.	.	.	.
Thomas Williams	13	8	6	14	2.0-8	1.0-7	.	.	.	.	.	.	.
Oscar Lua	13	8	5	13	1.0-1	.	.	.	.	.	.	.	.
Terrell Thomas	11	7	2	9	.	.	2-29	2	.	.	.	.	.
Josh Pinkard	13	6	3	9	.	.	.	.	.	1-0	1	.	.
Team	9	7	.	7	6.0-19	2.0-8	.	.	.	.	.	.	.
Ryan Ting	10	3	4	7	.	.	.	.	.	.	.	.	.

Player	GP	Solo	Ast	Total	TFl-Yds	No-Yds	Int-Yds	BrUp	QBH	Rcv-Yds	FF	Blkd Kick	Saf
Justin Tolliver	12	3	2	5	.	.	.	.	.	.	.	.	.
Desmond Reed	13	4	1	5	1.0-12	.	.	.	.	.	1	.	.
Greg Farr	8	3	1	4	.	.	.	.	.	.	.	.	.
John Walker	13	1	2	3	.	.	.	.	.	.	.	.	.
Ryan Killeen	13	3	.	3	.	.	.	.	.	.	.	.	.
Lee Webb	13	.	2	2	.	.	.	.	.	.	.	.	.
Sedrick Ellis	11	.	2	2	.	.	.	.	.	.	.	.	.
Sam Baker	13	2	.	2	.	.	.	.	.	.	.	.	.
Travis Tofi	5	1	1	2	.	.	.	.	.	.	.	.	.
LaJuan Ramsey	9	.	2	2	.	.	.	.	.	.	.	.	.
Alex Morrow	6	2	.	2	.	.	.	.	.	.	.	.	.
Alex Gomez	2	2	.	2	.	.	.	.	.	.	.	.	.
Mike Brittingham	10	1	.	1	.	.	.	.	.	.	.	.	.
Dale Thompson	12	.	1	1	.	.	.	.	.	.	.	.	.
Brandon Ting	12	.	1	1	.	.	.	.	.	.	.	.	.
John Drake	10	1	.	1	.	.	.	.	.	.	.	.	.
Steve Smith	8	1	.	1	.	.	.	.	.	.	1	.	.
Rashaad Goodrum	2	1	.	1	1.0-8	1.0-8	.	.	.	.	.	.	.
Hershel Dennis	9	1	.	1	.	.	.	.	.	.	.	.	.
Dominique Byrd	9	1	.	1	.	.	.	.	.	.	.	.	.
David Kirtman	13	.	1	1	.	.	.	.	.	.	.	.	.
Greig Carlson	11	1	.	1	.	.	.	.	.	.	.	.	.
Fred Matua	13	.	.	.	.	.	.	.	.	1-0	.	.	.
Total	**13**	**501**	**304**	**805**	**120-522**	**50-344**	**22-358**	**59**	**9**	**16-32**	**21**	**1**	**.**
Opponents	**13**	**575**	**338**	**913**	**84-318**	**25-176**	**7-75**	**39**	**6**	**12-4**	**14**	**3**	**1**

The sports and photo staffs of the *Los Angeles Daily News, Long Beach Press-Telegram, San Gabriel Valley Tribune, Pasadena Star-News, Whittier Daily News, San Bernardino Sun, Inland Valley Daily Bulletin* and *Redlands Daily Facts* all contributed to the coverage of the Trojans' 2004 season. We gratefully acknowldedge the efforts of:

SPORTS STAFF

Doug Jacobs
Scott Wolf
Steve Dilbeck
Kevin Modesti
Rich Hammond
Rick Hazeltine
Jon Clifford
Matt McHale

PHOTOGRAPHY STAFF

Dean Musgrove
Terri Thuente
Roger Vargo
Roxanne Kotzman
Shane Michael Kidder
Michael Owen Baker
Hans Gutknecht
Andy Holzman
John Lazar
Will Lester
John McCoy
Tom Mendoza
John Valenzuela
Evan Yee